Paradise Found:

How To Live In North America's Best Climate For Under $300 A Month

By
R. Emil Neuman

Paradise Found:
How To Live In North America's Best Climate For Under $300 A Month

ISBN 0-9614924-0-6

Published By
United Research Publishers

Printed in U.S.A.

Dedication

To Mom, Dad and Debbie

*There is only today. Yesterday is a
cancelled check. Tomorrow is a
sum owed you.*

Contents

Introduction

Ever dreamed of a better place...a place where the climate is perfect year round...prices are ridiculously cheap...where people are warm and friendly...no crime or pollution... no congestion or crowds...a place only a few hours from America where 30,000 Americans are already enjoying the "good life".

A place where you can turn away from the stress and tension of modern life and live comfortably for under $300 a month.

That's why I call this book "Paradise Found"....it's the closest thing to paradise you'll ever find. I've traveled through Europe, the Carribbean and Hawaii and never have I seen a place with such enchanting beauty, low prices and perpetual summer climate. A place where you can say good-bye to tension and high living costs.

Is this place for everyone? No. Absolutely not. But if you're looking for a low-cost vacation spot, a place to get away from blistering cold winters, or a place to retire...this paradise has something for you.

Life is short. The average life-span is only about 25,550 days. That's right, 25,550 days...that's if you're lucky enough to live to be 70. How many days have you used up? How many precious days do you have left?

This book tells you how to start enjoying life now in the world's best climate. The book explains all you need to know. How to get there, where to stay, where to eat, what to see and do. The book explains how to buy a home, how to earn extra money and feel right at home.

Most important the book shows you how to enjoy the good life on a poor-man's budget as 30,000 Americans are already doing.

Telephone Call:
Detroit To San Diego
Middle of January

"Rog, this is your Dad calling, how are things in San Diego?"

"Just great, how's everything back in Detroit?"

"Well that's why I'm calling--things could be a lot better. First of all, I've had it with this Michigan weather. It's freezing cold here again. The snow's practically up to my ass. Couldn't get out of the driveway this morning. So I'm stuck here in the house until the plow truck comes."

"You know Rog, I'm really depressed. When I retired 7 years ago I never planned on staying in this place. I've always hated this bone-chilling cold even as a kid. But here I am almost 70 and still here freezing my ass off."

"Dad, I've been telling you for years to move to San Diego."

"Heck, you know I can't afford it out there in California. You have to be a millionaire just to survive. Besides your mother doesn't like California. Come to think of it she doesn't like Florida either. Of course I can understand why she doesn't like Florida. The last few trips there I froze my fanny off. Seems like everyone is saying the same thing about Florida. You can't count on sunshine anymore. Then in the summer it's too hot. Besides it's getting awfully crowded there. And it's not as cheap as it used to be."

"Then you have all those old people. I know I'm near 70, but those people in Florida are either walking with a cane or being pushed around in a wheelchair. I've got a lot of good years left in me, and seeing older people in this condition depresses me."

1

"I'm just grateful to have my retirement pension, and social security coming in every month. It's not a lot of money, but we seem to manage as long as we watch every penny. But every year it's getting harder and harder to make ends meet."

"The heating bills are a real problem. Rog, you know I'm paying over $100 a week just to heat the house. Heck, when I retired I could heat the place for a fraction of that. The taxes are killing us too. I'm paying over $3000 a year on my little house."

"You know, I feel overwhelmed with it all. The cold weather, heating bills, taxes and inflation. I just wish there was a way out. I feel helpless. Heck, I can't control the weather, the taxes, the prices. Nothing. There's got to be something better than this. Some place where I'm not being kicked in the ass by butt-freezing weather and pocket-jolting living costs."

I knew exactly what Dad was feeling. I felt the same way about Detroit before I left for San Diego in 1978. I worked as a Congressional Investigator for 12 years. Drove to downtown Detroit every day. I can remember the blistering cold. Getting up early in the morning. Scraping snow off the windows. Waiting for the car to heat up and shivering all the way to work. I remember the icy, hazardous roads and getting to work half exhausted. Never seeing the sun. Getting to work when it's dark, and leaving when it's dark. The only thing that kept me going was the dream of one day being able to break away. And finally I did--to San Diego, California.

But I was lucky. I'd make a few bucks and was able to make the break from Detroit. Dad, on the other hand, is living on a pension. He isn't in a financial position to break away.

Frankly, I didn't have the guts to tell Dad things

looked bleak for him. That after working his ass off at Ford Motor Company for 40 years, he was stuck in Detroit in knee-deep snow, paying through the nose to keep the house warm. There had to be more to life. But what was I going to tell him to lessen these realities? I had to come up with something fast. But what?

Then it hit me. My neighbor Kay, a widow in her 50's, keeps telling me about a paradise called Lake Chapala, about 30 miles from Guadalajara, Mexico. A place she visits twice a year, and plans to retire. I've heard so much about the place--the perfect climate, the cheap prices--I feel like I've been there. Whenever she starts talking about Lake Chapala, I can't shut her up.

So I decided to mention it to Dad just to get his reaction. I'd tell him more if he seemed interested. I figured this would be better than painting a hopeless picture of his situation.

So I started, "Dad have you ever heard of Lake Chapala, near Guadalajara, Mexico?"

"Well, I've heard of Guadalajara, there are about 30,000 or so Americans living there. I've always wanted to go there and check it out, but I can't get anyone to go with me."

I could hear a little interest, even excitement, in his voice so I took the opportunity to pound away on what my neighbor told me about Lake Chapala.

"Dad, Lake Chapala is the largest lake in Mexico. It is nestled in the mountains about 5100 feet above sea level. The lake stretches a full 60 miles and is about 17 miles at it's widest point."

"The climate there is perfect--the best climate in the world. It stays around 75 degrees year round. It very seldom rains, and the nights are nice and cool so you can sleep."

"The scenery will take your breath away. The sparkling blue lake surrounded by green mountains, red, yellow and pink flowers, blue skies and a never-ending crisp breeze from the lake."

Aside from the weather, I knew the cost of living was the most important factor to Dad, so I really hammered away here.

"The prices in Lake Chapala are so low, they're almost ridiculous. Luxurious hotel rooms are $7.00 a night. Full course dinners $1.75 to $2.50. You can live like a virtual millionaire for about $300 to $400 a month."

"Wages there are cheap--about .50 cents per hour. Most Americans have a cook, housekeeper and gardner."

"How many Americans did you say are living around Lake Chapala?" Dad probed."

"About 30,000. That's just Americans. There are many Canadians and a few German and British there too."

Dad seemed a little skeptical.

"You know this paradise you are describing here is a bit hard to believe. You know everyone is looking for a place like that. A perfect climate, cheap prices, scenery and all. I'd have to see the place for myself."

I seized on the opportunity.

"Well let's go there and either confirm the place as a paradise or write it off as a bunch of bullshit. If nothing else you will be able to catch a few rays of sun there."

"When do you want to go?" Dad said.

"How about February 15th?" I replied. "I'll catch a flight to Guadalajara and meet you there. We can rent a car at the airport and drive up to Lake Chapala."

"It's a deal."

Before hanging up Dad said, "You know I feel a lot

better about things now. I'm glad I called.See you in paradise."

I sat by the phone awhile thinking maybe I built up Dad's hopes too high with the idea of Lake Chapala. I gave him a lot of second-hand information. I believed my neighbor is honest and trustworthy. But maybe her concept of Paradise is different than ours.

Whatever the situation, few people are better qualified than me to find the truth about Lake Chapala. For 12 years I worked as an Investigator for the United States Congress. During that time I won several awards for my investigative reports. I am not bragging mind you. I was good because I worked hard at it. I'd go that extra mile to get the facts. I've always believed that finding truth is like peeling an onion. You have to keep peeling to get at the real truth. I don't believe anything until I see the proof.

As for formal education, I'm a graduate accountant with a BS Degree. I sat for the CPA exam, scoring in the top 5% of all candidates. I've always welcomed a challange and I was determined to go to Lake Chapala and get the real story.

It seemed like a tough job, but someone had to do it.

Journey To Paradise:
Meeting at Guadalajara Airport

Stepping off the plane in Guadalajara I was met with a comforting blast of warm air that instantly made me feel good.

The first thing I noticed about the terrain around the airport was how much it looked like Hawaii. This is a mountainous region with deep green colors spattered with red and white flowers.

I met Dad at the airport as planned. We rented a volkswagon 4-door and started on our journey to Lake Chapala.

From the airport, Lake Chapala is about 19 miles. By cab it costs about $9.00. The price is the same no matter how many people are in the cab. So if 4 people take the ride the cost is only $2.25 a person.

The road to Lake Chapala is decent. It had two wide lanes in amazingly good repair even by U.S. standards. Traffic was moderate with a roaring truck or bus passing by now and then. As we continued on the Road to Lake Chapala, you noticed more cars being replaced by people on horseback. You could see tiny wagons carrying wood replacing noisy trucks and busses. You sensed you were leaving the outskirts of the city and getting closer to green mountains and a more peaceful place.

Dad commented how comfortable the temperature was--a pleasant 75°. We had the windows down. I could tell Dad was really enjoying the climate. Detroit was below zero when he boarded the plane.

"Shouldn't be long now," Dad commented.

We were both a little excited knowing that at any moment Lake Chapala would be in sight. Then as we turned a sharp bend we saw off in the distance a large crystal lake nestled in the high green mountains. It was an impressive sight. It reminded me of Lake Tahoe, the vacation mecca on the California boarder.

Lake Chapala is the largest lake in Mexico. It winds 60 miles through the Sierra Madre mountains. At its widest point it spans 17 miles. But its narrowest point is less than 4 miles across.

The Lake supports a wide variety of fish and wild birds. The most popular fish is the Lake Chapala white fish. It is proudly advertised on menus in local restaurants.

Lake Chapala is a sanctuary for wild birds of all sizes and colors from around the world. You can see thousands of birds here. Song birds, hummingbirds, even tropical parrots. Sighting a snow white goose or black raven is common. Once in a while you can even see a brilliantly colored cockatoo.

The climate at Lake Chapala is best described as "perpetual summer". You're always comfortable because constant breezes come in from the Lake. It's often called the world's best climate. The warmest months are April and May with an average high temperature of 85°. The average low for these months is about 65°, making it comfortable for sleeping.

The "cooler" months are November through February, when the average high is 76°. The average low is a comfortable 58°.

Lake Chapala enjoys a rainy season from mid-June through September when the surrounding mountains explode into color. During this period you can expect rain nearly every day. Fortunately, the rain rarely interferes with your daily activities since it nearly always comes late in the evening while you are indoors or sleeping. In fact, many residents say some of their best sleeping hours have come during the rainy season.

Discovery of this mountain/lake paradise is not new to Americans. Wealthy Americans visited Lake Chapala in the late 1800's. Many Americans built homes and spent part of each year on the Lake. For example, Albert Braniff, founder of Braniff Airlines, built a large home near the Lake in about 1885. Tennessee Williams reportedly spent a good deal of time here writing many of his famous novels.

In the 1900's Lake Chapala was on its way to becoming an American tourist playground. But the Mexican Civil War scared most Americans away from the Lake (and Mexico overall).

The region has changed little since Tennessee Williams roamed around the Lake dreaming up ideas for his books.

* * *

Before long we were driving down a sloping curve toward the town of Chapala. This is a quaint little village right on the western shore of the Lake.

Driving down the main street of Chapala you could see people sitting or strolling the boulevard that divides the road. Looking toward the center of town you can see the Lake encircled by mountains. I commented to Dad about the striking beauty of the place. Dad nodded and just kept staring straight ahead at the colorful scenery.

Driving further, we spotted the town square where townspeople come at night to sit and relax. The Catholic Church, an impressive spectacle for such a small town, is next. The church is the center of activity. Some kind of function takes place there every night.

At the end of Chapala is a park by the Lake. There is also a pier where you can walk out about 150 feet onto the Lake. Small fishing boats are docked around the pier. Fishermen take out these boats in the early morning hours. Fresh fish from the Lake is a basic staple of the local people.

Sightseeing boats are available for hire to cruise around the Lake.

I anxiously parked the car. Dad and I walked through the park looking out at the Lake and mountains. The weather was perfect, about 75° with a crisp breeze gently blowing in from the Lake.

Sitting there I felt relaxed. An almost carefree feeling came over my body.

Dad said, "Nice, isn't it?"

As time went by we realized we needed a place to stay for the night.

Dad said, "Let's find an American and get a recommendation."

We walked over to the pier and saw a fella about 70 years old standing by himself. Dad said, "How long have you been here in Chapala?"

"About 1 month and I'm never leaving. Hey, my name is Jack from Tampa, Florida, what's your's?"

Jack was 73. He had been a sailor most of his life after serving in the Navy during World War II. He heard about Chapala while sailing near Barbados in the West Indies four years ago. He bought a one-way ticket to Chapala after getting fed up with retirement in Florida.

"It's too darn cold in Florida," Jack muttered. "I got fed up with all the old people there. Besides the prices are getting so high my pension barely covered necessities. Then my wife--a 30 year old gal--up and divorced me and took about all I had. That's when I decided to come here."

For 73 Jack was in remarkable shape. He was tall and lean with a slim waist and broad shoulders.

Jack continued, "I got me a nice place about 2 miles west of here. Only $150 a month. Nice place. Two beds, full cooking facilities, a courtyard, laundry area, big swimming pool out front."

"Figure I can live here for under $300 a month. I mean good living too. Better than I could live in Florida for $1300 a month. And the climate here is perfect. I mean it's predictable. You know it's about 75° every day."

Dad asked Jack why he needed 2 beds in his apartment.

Jack answered, "I've got no family. Most of my close friends died off on me. I've really got no one left. Would be sort of nice to find a senorita as a companion."

Jack told us one of the nicest places in the area was the Hotel Real de Chapala. He said it was on the Lake about 6 miles west of Chapala.

We said goodbye to Jack and started driving toward the Hotel Real de Chapala.

Hotel Real de Chapala

When we drove onto the hotel grounds the front looked like an average motel. So with low expectations we asked the desk clerk to show us a room.

The desk clerk led us through a huge courtyard with dozens of giant eucalyptus trees, red and yellow flowers and green tropical plants.

"Do you want an upstairs or downstairs room Senor?"

Figuring that with the downstairs room we could sit out by the Lake, Dad said, "Is the downstairs room the same price?"

"Si Senor," the desk clerk replied.

"Okay, we'll see the downstairs room," Dad insisted.

When the clerk opened the door, I couldn't believe how big the room was. It was 2 to 3 times the size of an "average motel room" in the states. The room had two huge double beds and a cozy living room area. It had a couch, table and two lounge chairs. Large sliding glass doors opened to a courtyard that led out to the Lake.

I looked out at the Lake with the green mountains

A view of the front of the Hotel Real de Chapala. As you drive in, you'll see colorful flowers and trees. In the background are the beautiful mountains that surround the Lake.

A back view of the Hotel Real de Chapala. This hotel is owned by the University of Guadalajara. Many medical doctors come here from Guadalajara for the weekend. The hotel has about 80 rooms. Half of the rooms front the Lake. The other half face a beautiful garden with tall Eucalyptus trees. This is one of the nicest hotels at Lake Chapala.

A view of the hallway leading to the rooms at the Hotel Real de Chapala.

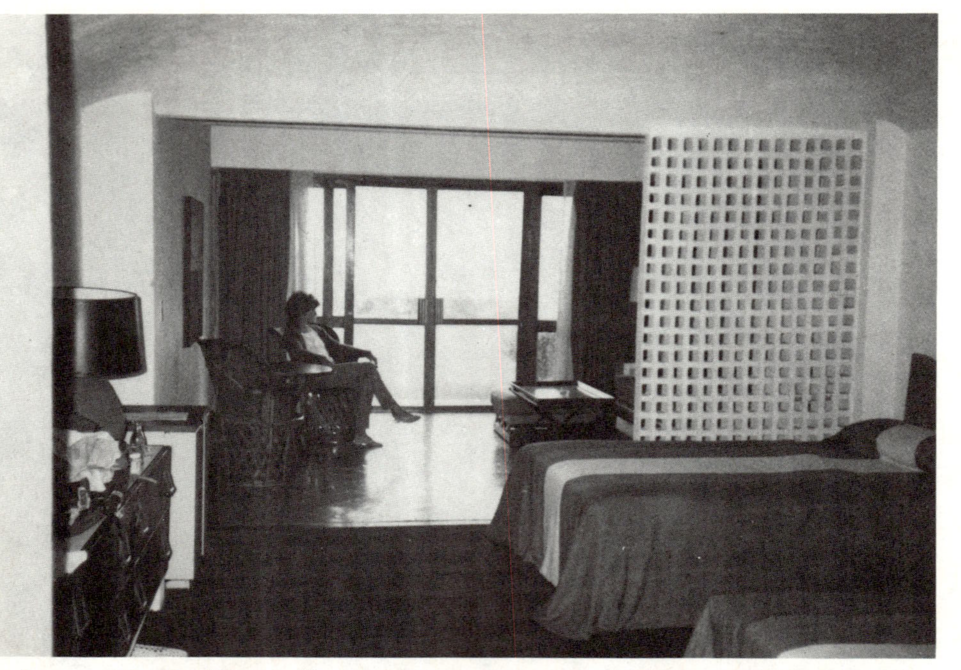

A room at the Hotel Real de Chapala. The rooms are mammoth. They are probably about 600 square feet. The sliding glass doors open onto a courtyard that leads to the Lake. The Hotel Real de Chapala is one of the nicest places to stay in the lake Chapala area. The girl is my wife Debbie.

The garden area in the back of the Hotel Real de Chapala. In front of the chairs is a garden eating area. Every Sunday the hotel hosts a Mexican buffet that is very popular with Americans and Canadians.

shooting up toward the sky. I thought of when I paid $160 a night for a room in Hawaii half this size, and not as nice. I figured this room was worth at least $50 a night even in Mexico.

"How much?" Dad questioned.

"Senor, we are having a promotion now. The room is $9.50 a piece per night."

I saw a look of disbelief on Dad's face. Dad repeated, "You said this room is $9.50 a piece per night? Okay, we'll take it."

We settled in quickly not wanting to waste any time before exploring the grounds.

Opening the sliding glass doors we stepped out onto a rich green lawn with five foot high shrubs on either side which provided privacy from the other units.

"Let's walk over to the pool," Dad suggested.

I was stunned by the beauty of the place. It looked a little like my vision of Paradise. Full green trees with colorful flowers. White flowers, pink, red, orange. The aroma of flowers was almost intoxicating. I never thought so many flowers could grow in any one place.

The pool was large, surrounded by white wrought-iron tables and chairs. Tropical green plants and low-hanging shade trees were growing everywhere.

"Wouldn't it be nice to eat here in the garden?" I suggested.

"Sure would," Dad said, "Let's do it."

The Restaurant

"Welcome Senors--two persons?"

"Yes, could we have that table under the big shade tree by the pool?"

A view of the pool and lakeside area at the Hotel Real de Chapala. The hotel has an outside bar near the pool.

"Si Senor, follow me."

Once seated, Dad looked at the menu and said, "Gosh, the one-half barbeque chicken dinner is less than $2.00. And it comes with salad, rice, french fries or baked potatoes and vegetables. How could this be?"

"Hey, let's reserve judgment until we finish eating," I responded.

One thing you have to get used to in Lake Chapala is the slow pace of life. This slow pace is most noticed in restaurants. Typically you can expect to wait a minimum of 20 minutes to get served. As for the check, it won't come until you ask for it. You could sit at your table all day and no check will come. So if you're in a hurry, it's a good idea to ask for the check when you get your order.

"Looks good," Dad said as the waiter placed on our table two plates of golden brown, barbequed chicken with crisp green salad and fluffy rice. I had a cold beer with the meal.

Mexico is noted for its fine beer. The main brands are Tecate, Carta Blanca and Superior. My favorite is Tecate. It's made in a small Mexican town called Tecate, only a few miles from San Diego, California.

"How's your chicken?" Dad questioned.

"Fantastic," I responded.

We both agreed everything was almost too good to be true. The food, the service, the room--everything was excellent.

As we sat there chatting in this magnificent garden setting, the red-toned sun slowly slipped behind the purple mountains. The temperature was perfect with a cooling breeze off the Lake adding that extra something that made you feel good all over. Glad to be alive!

At that moment we both sensed we were onto

This cobblestone walkway leads down to the Lake from the back of the Hotel Real de Chapala. The structure at the front of the Lake is a fish house. Local fishermen catch fish by the Lake and then use the house to clean them.

something here. Maybe we had stumbled onto a paradise. But, I'm skeptical. I wanted more facts about this Lake Chapala before I would concede anything. I wanted to talk to some Americans who have actually lived here for a number of years. I wanted to find out all the negatives of living here. All the problems. I have done a fair amount of travel in my time. I know you can get a great first impression of a place. Then, once you see the tourist attractions, there is nothing left.

So before I made final judgment on Lake Chapala, I wanted to find out more. I was determined to uncover the truth.

Next morning we had breakfast at the hotel. We ate in a cozy enclosed dinning room just off the pool. Dad had pancakes with pure maple syrup and coffee. I had eggs, bacon, toast and coffee. The total bill: $3.00.

There are dozens of little towns surrounding Lake Chapala. But only two main towns have a high concentration of Americans: Chapala and Ajijic (Ah He Hic). Both towns are located on the west shore of the Lake about five miles apart. Of the approximate 4,000 Americans living around the lake, most live in these two towns.

Ajijic

This quaint little town is the hub of American (and Canadian) activity. Down its narrow cobblestone streets you'll find an American library full of books and magazines written in English. The library is operated by a small staff of American volunteers. Ajijic also houses an American cultural center run by American volunteers.

A street in Ajijic that peers down toward the Lake. This is one of many streets around the Lake that make this area one of the most picturesque in the world.

Another pretty, winding cobblestone street that goes down toward the Lake.

Ajijic is a mecca for American artists. One or two strolls down a cobblestone street or a visit to the town square will certainly bring you in contact with an American artist, writer, poet or philosopher.

Once you see this tiny Mexican village you'll understand what draws so many Americans here as permanent residents. A relaxing walk through the clean narrow side streets exposes you to little shops selling leather goods, local art and jewelry. You can stop at one of the many little restaurants, have lunch or a cooling drink.

The most popular restaurant and "watering hole" in Ajijic is a lake-side place called the Posada. The Posada is owned by a former restaurateur from Canada and his Mexican wife. The food is American style, and very reasonable.

On almost any day of the week the Posada is filled with Americans and Canadians. The Posada is also a popular night spot for dinner, dancing and conversation. During the day it's the place to go for a refreshing drink while gazing out on the Lake and surrounding mountains.

On the western section of Ajijic is an American-style community of 100 or more Americans and Canadians.

Meeting The Permanent American Residents

While cruising through the American section of Ajijic we met a personable American named Fred.

"Can I help you fellows?" Fred asked as we were creeping slowly down a cobblestone street in our Volkswagon.

This is a residential street in Ajijic. Behind those modest walls are mansions that front the Lake. Many of these homes are between 3,000 and 6,000 square feet. Most of the homes have a pool and a large courtyard. It's hard to believe that such mansions are behind these modest-looking walls and cobblestone streets.

"Is this a private street?" I probed.

"No, No," Fred answered. "I just want to know if I can help in some way. You know, answer any questions. I can see you are Americans and new here."

Fred was about 53, a retired Army sergeant. He had been living in Ajijic for 15 years.

I took Fred up on his offer to answer questions. "Why are you here at Lake Chapala and not retired in Florida or California?"

Fred explained that Lake Chapala had the best climate in the world, saying, "I'm never too hot, never too cold. Always perfectly comfortable."

Fred told us he couldn't possibly live on a retired sergeant's pension in the U.S. "I get about $600 a month and live like a king here. I have a cook, housekeeper and gardener. Try that in the U.S. and see what it costs you."

Fred went on to say he has no regrets spending the last 15 years here. "I love the Mexican people, they're mild mannered and kind. The Americans living here are great too. A lot of socializing goes on. Parties, get-togethers, and outings. Being here in Mexico, you have a common bond with other Americans. You get to know each other real fast and maintain close friendships. Back in the states, you could live on the same block with someone and never know their name."

Fred invited us into his house saying, "You fellas can see how we live here on $600 a month. That's $300 a month each for me and my wife."

The house was about half a block from the Lake. It was a Spanish style, meaning it was built around a courtyard. The home was nice and cozy with three large bedrooms and about 1500 square feet of living space. I figured a home like this in the U.S. would cost at least $100,000. About $150,000 or more in California.

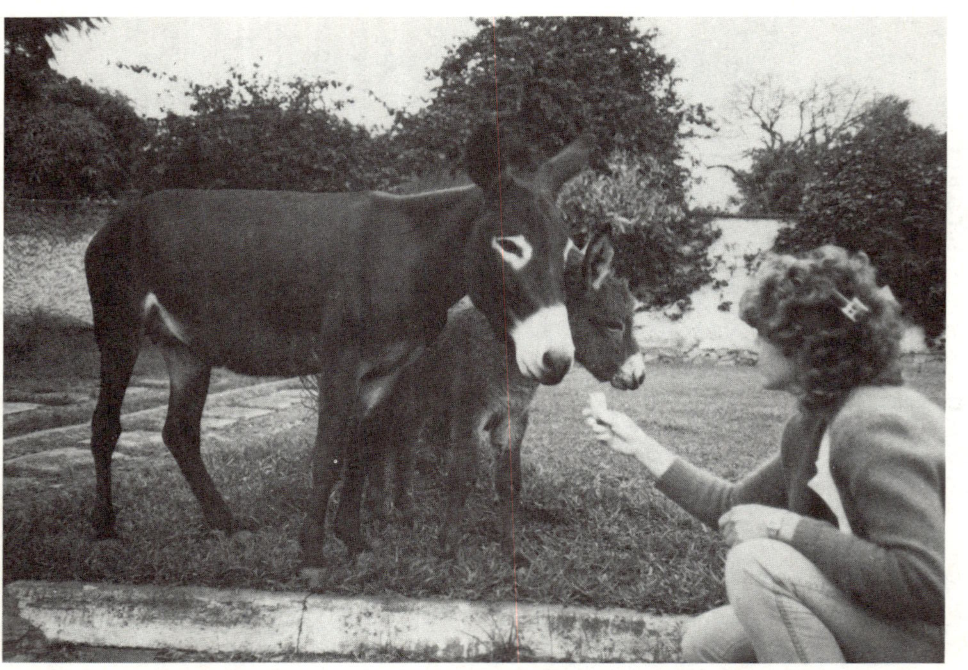

My wife Debbie feeding one of the many buros living wild in the Lake Chapala area. These animals roam around and co-exist with man without any problem whatsoever.

"How much are your property taxes here?" Dad asked.

"About $70 a year."

"A year?" Dad probed.

"That is right, a year," Fred responded.

I could see the look of envy on Dad's face. He is always complaining about his property taxes. Dad pays over $3000 a year for a house the size of Fred's.

"How about utilities?" I continued.

"Oh about $4 a month for everything--gas, electricity and water," Fred answered.

We walked into the kitchen where Fred introduced Margaret his wife who was preparing lunch. Next to her, peeling potatoes, was a Mexican girl about 18 years old.

"How do you like it here in Lake Chapala?" I asked Margaret.

"I love it here," she replied. "Went back to Texas for a few weeks last month and I couldn't wait to get back."

"Don't you ever get bored?" I probed.

"Never," she replied. "I'm always busy."

She went on to explain how she is involved in various benefits and fund-raising events to help the local townspeople.

"There is the golf club, the sewing club, the bridge club, the square dance club, the library club."

Fred broke in saying, "Don't forget the American Legion and Elks club."

Fred took us out to the court yard. We saw the Mexican gardener edging the grass and weeding the flower garden.

"What do you have to pay your help?" Dad asked.

"Oh, about 52 cents an hour, and that is good wages for this area."

Fred went on to explain that Mexicans living in

Chapala and Ajijic are much better off economically than surrounding villages. That's because Americans provide a large number of jobs.

"Everyone I know has a housekeeper and gardener and many have a cook and full-time babysitter," Fred explained.

Fred went on to say, "Americans actually pay a little more than the going wages in other nearby towns. Because of this, there is no resentment toward Americans whatsoever. In fact, the Mexican people love Americans."

As Fred was talking I reflected on how comfortable I felt here at Lake Chapala. I couldn't recall one bad incident. Not even one bad look or wisecrack from any Mexican. This was true even with teenagers and younger kids. I felt welcome. Like the Mexican people wanted me to be here.

While I stood there dreaming, one of Fred's neighbors named Tom stopped by to borrow a hammer.

Tom had lived here in the Lake Chapala area for 7 years. A retired truck driver. Tom was about 55.

His visit gave me another opportunity to find out more about any bad aspects of life at Lake Chapala. So I asked Tom, "Why do you choose to live here instead of somewhere else?"

"Tried Hawaii, too expensive. Same with California. Florida's too darn cold in the winter, unbelievably hot in the summer. Climate here is perfect. Probably the world's best. It's because of the elevation you know. You're up 5100 feet here. Sea level would be miserably hot this time of year," Tom explained. "You never need air conditioning here and heat is needed only a few weeks in the winter. Heat and all other utilities are less than $5 a month. Taxes for the entire year are $27--what did you pay last year?" Tom asked in a boastful way.

You could see the sincerity and enthusiasm in Tom's face as he continued, "I live here like a king on about $600 a month. I've got my own cook, gardener and maid. My wife loves it here too. We visited her family in New York last Christmas and couldn't wait to get back."

I could see that Tom would spend the whole day raving about Lake Chapala so I interrupted and asked, "What are the two things you dislike most about the area?"

There was a moment of silence then Tom stuttered out, "You know I can't think of one darn thing I don't like about this place."

Tom thought again and explained that Lake Chapala is a paradise now, but he is afraid too many Americans will find out about the place and turn it into a tourist area.

Tom explained too many Americans could put pressure on the low prices. "If too many American greenbacks are spread around, this whole cheap way of life here could collapse. You would have another Acapulco," Tom said.

Before leaving with the borrowed hammer, Tom said, "Fellas, don't go back and tell too many people about our little paradise here."

Americans In Mexico

You already know that about 30,000 Americans live near Lake Chapala. But overall, it's estimated that over 1 million Americans live in Mexico. This is just Americans. It doesn't include Canadians or other nationalities. One million. That's a lot of Americans. It's more than the combined population of Wyoming, Vermont and Nevada. There are more Americans living in Mexico than any other place in the world other than the U.S. itself.

What type of Americans live in Mexico? Well, it's pretty much of a cross section of American society-- jetsetters, writers, artists, students and retired persons.

Retired persons represent the largest segment of Americans living in Mexico. Retired persons in Mexico probably represent about 70 percent of all Americans. You have retired executives, retired postmen, people living on social security and pensions. Many live off interest on money deposited in a U.S. bank. The "typical" retired American in Mexico is young, probably 60 years old.

The second largest group of Americans living in Mexico are those working for large U.S. Corporations like General Motors, Ford, IBM, and Burroughs. These Americans work mostly in large cities like Guadalajara or Mexico City. Mexican companies also employ Americans. This requires special permission from the Mexican Government. Most Americans work as consultants and technicians where a specific skill is lacking among Mexican nationals.

There is a misconception that foreign companies operating in Mexico are primarily owned by Mexicans. This is true only for certain kinds of businesses like broadcasting, publishing and mining. Many companies operating in Mexico are 100 percent foreign owned. For example, Ford and General Motors operate in Mexico yet have no Mexican ownership. Likewise Volkswagon operates its largest factory in Mexico which is totally German owned. The Mexican government encourages U.S. companies to operate in Mexico. The purpose of this policy is to bolster the economy and make more jobs available to Mexicans.

Students and creative persons like writers and artists are the next largest group of Americans living in Mexico.

Over the years thousands of American students have attended the University of Guadalajara Medical School. It's no secret that U.S. medical colleges are often over crowded. This means qualified students sometimes must wait years for admittance. So rather than "wait away" precious time, many students come to Mexico for medical training.

Many creative persons live in Mexico because of the tax advantages (and low living costs). An American living in Mexico is not subject to Mexican taxes on income derived outside Mexico. So a writer living and writing in Mexico does not have to pay Mexican taxes if all written work is sold in the U.S. What's more, there are substantial U.S. tax advantages for writers and other creative persons who work and live in Mexico. The I.R.S. Publication No. 54, *Tax Guide for U.S. Citizens Abroad,* provides a good deal of information on the subject.

One last thought. Mexican law prohibits tourists from working while in Mexico. This law is enforced. The only exception is tourists working in the creative arts.

Writers, artists and composers may work at their craft with a tourist card as long as their work is sold outside Mexico. That's why so many Hollywood movies are filmed in Mexico. Creative work is done in Mexico but not sold there. The Mexican Government figures the creative work contributes to the nation's culture but does not interfere with opportunities available to Mexican nationals.

About The Tiny Mexican Towns
On The Lake

The tiny towns around the Lake are well-planned to meet the needs of the people. Most everything needed to live a comfortable life can be found in the town.

The Town Market

Every town has a market place where townspeople can buy fresh, low-cost food products. The markets are located near the center of town making shopping convenient and within walking distance of most everyone.

The wide-variety of foods available in these marketplaces is amazing. You will find a wide selection of fresh vegetables, fruits, grains, fresh fish, poultry, beef and pork. The market in Chapala even has a small restaurant area where you can sit and eat meals prepared with the fresh produce sold at the market.

If you are into health, you'll be able to get a selection of juices made fresh right before your eyes. I personally enjoyed a glass of carrot juice and later apple juice made from fresh apples.

Dad and I both love poultry, so we were glad to see crisp golden brown chicken turning on a rotisserie at the market. The price for a whole chicken is less than $1.00. And these chickens are all corn-fed--free of the chemicals put in U.S. feed.

While at the market place, Dad commented that if a person were to eat only the products sold here, they would be a lot healthier. "All that processed junk--TV dinners, canned goods, hot dogs with nitrates--just poisons people," Dad insisted.

In addition to the main market-place, each town has

The Lake Chapala market. Here you can get a veriety of fresh fruits and vegetables at ridiculously low prices. You can also get fresh meat, fish and barbequed chickens. The market has a small restaurant where you can get lunches and fresh juices.

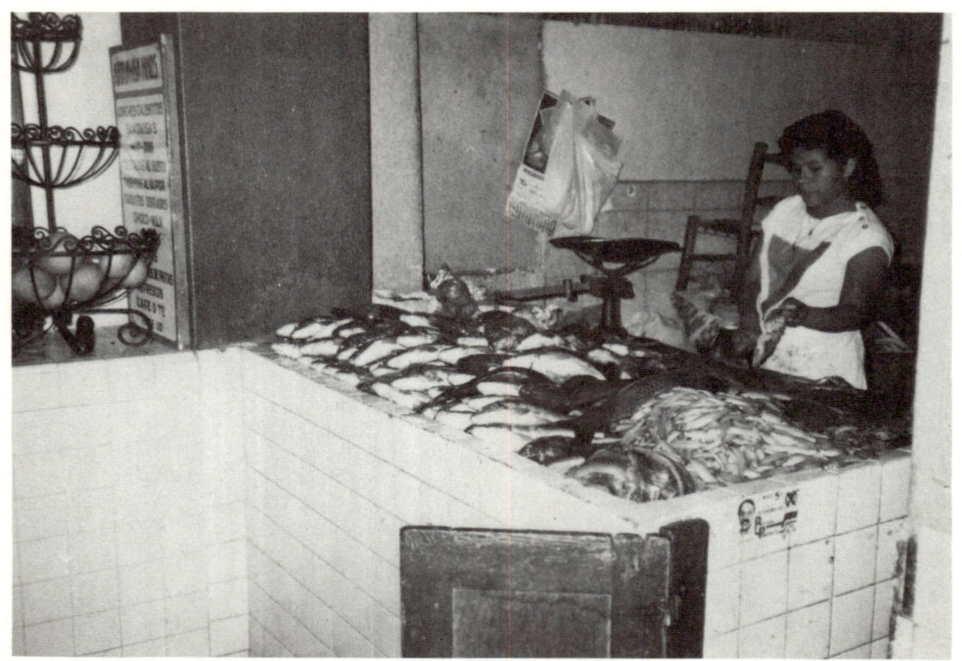

At the Chapala town market you can get a veriety of fresh fish and shellfish.

The shopping area along side of the town square in Chapala. Here you can get a variety of hand-crafted goods including leather, pottery and onyx. These little shops stay open 7 days a week. The prices are very reasonable.

smaller markets located a few blocks from one another. These smaller markets carry a more limited selection of products. From these smaller markets anyone can get basic food items within a short walk from home. This is especially convenient for the older residents of the town.

The Church

The church is a major part of the townspeople's lives. Almost every night some kind of activity is going on there. These meetings serve as a binding force to the townspeople. The church takes care of the spiritual needs of the town and guides people toward Christian behavior.

The churches are magnificent structures for these tiny towns. On the outside each church has its own unique design. On the inside too, you'll find unique local sculptures and paintings. Most churches around Lake Chapala were built over 200 year ago. For example, the church in Ajijic was built in 1740.

The Town Square

Every town has a square located in the center of town. The town square is designed to satisfy the town's social needs.

At any time day or night you can see people of all ages sitting on the benches talking to their neighbors. Others sit quietly enjoying the mild climate and watching children playing.

Don't be surprised to see one or two town dogs lounging around the square.

A view of the inside of the Church in Ajijic. Every town has a magnificent Church like this one. This Church was built in about 1740. The Church is the center of the town's activities.

A view of the inside of the Church at Ajijic. This is a magnificent statue on one of the side walls of the Church.

The town square in Chapala. The town square is the center of the town's activities. People come here to socialize and talk about matters that affect the town. Right behind the town square is the town market and shopping area.

The Appeal Of Lake Chapala

Aside from the near perfect climate, the sheer beauty of the place and the low prices, there is a strong appeal here at Lake Chapala that attracts Americans.

That appeal is the simplicity of life and the low stress that simplicity brings. Almost every aspect of living here is simple. The area is free of traffic and congestion. There are no factories anywhere near the Lake. So you are free of pollution and the health problems filthy air brings. There is no population problem. So you are free of crowded conditions and the stress brought about by people in competition for restaurant tables, parking and accommodations.

The times I have driven to Los Angeles on business I returned to San Diego exhausted. The conditions in that large city are beyond belief.

At times the smog is so bad you can just barely make out traffic signs. The air quality is so terrible your eyes burn and become red and sore. You can actually taste the air and your throat becomes raw from normal breathing.

Traffic can be so bad around Los Angeles that a 10 mile trip to work can take up to one hour. And when you look around at other drivers you can see the pent-up anger and frustration in their faces. They have turned over control of their life to traffic jams and congestion. And in return then get a good dose of stress--both mental and physical, each day of their life.

How many years of life does this kind of stress take off a person's life? Who can say for sure.

The lack of stress and anger at Lake Chapala shows on people's faces. Faces here look content, fulfilled and relaxed.

I am getting my shoes shined in Chapala. A shine costs about 40¢. That's what it cost in the U.S. about 30 years ago.

Drugs, booze and other excesses are not a problem here. You can be in the heart of town or walk down the darkest street and you won't see a single derelict sprawled out in doorways or sidewalks.

On a recent trip to San Francisco I could not believe the number of people I saw sleeping in the streets. I am talking about thousands of people. Street after street was carpeted with people in need of help.

There is virtually no crime here at Lake Chapala. I've been all over the world and I don't believe I have felt more safe or secure anywhere. I have walked down the darkest street in Chapala and Ajijic with no sense of fear for my safety whatsoever.

Poverty

The Mexican people at Lake Chapala cherish older things more than new things. For example old appliances, furniture and even clothing often sell for more than new items. That is hard for many Americans to understand because we have become used to our "throw away" life style.

The Mexican fondness for the "older" rather than the "new" can best be seen in the condition of the outside of homes and businesses around the Lake. Mexican homes often seem in need of paint and repair by American standards. But a close look at the exterior of these homes reveals that a single coat of paint--an hour or two work--would have these homes looking like "new". Of course the Mexican people don't want them looking that way.

The older, "need-of-repair" look of structures in Mexican towns is often seen by Americans as poverty or

Here a man rides a donkey down a street in Ajijic. Man and animal seem to co-exist very well.

Being at Lake Chapala is like going back in time 150 years or more. Down the cobblestone streets you can still see men riding donkeys.

even filth. Nothing could be further from the truth. It is simply that the Mexican people have different values about new and old.

While the outside of homes may look "unkept" by American standards, the insides are spotless in almost every case. Here too, older furniture and household items are more prized than the new.

The Children Of Lake Chapala

The strict standards of cleanliness in the Mexican people can be seen in the appearance of the children. The children are dressed up like little dolls. Spotlessly clean.

For example, little girls typically wear colorful dresses, white socks and patent leather shoes. Their shiny black hair is finely groomed and often braided in pigtails. When they smile their bright white teeth are a pleasing contrast to their bronze skin.

Whenever I see these little dolls walking down the cobblestone streets I marvel at how their mothers find time and patience to keep them looking so tidy. Even more baffling is how the children manage to stay away from mud.

Self Reliance

There is no welfare in Mexico. No food stamps, public housing, unemployment compensation or AFDC. When the people of Lake Chapala need help they turn to family not the government. Those with no

You see a large number of children in the Lake Chapala area. Here are two girls waiting for their mother to finish shopping at the Chapala market.

Many children and adults sell home made products on the streets of Chapala. Here is a little girl selling home-baked cookies.

All up and down the cobblestone streets of these little towns you can see pretty little girls in the doorways. Here are two of the cutest girls you'll ever see.

family get help from the church.

Without the presence of big government people seem to have a sense of self-reliance and control over their lives.

You don't see people in need of food. You won't see people rummaging through trash cans like you routinely see in downtown Los Angeles or other large cities.

The Women Of Lake Chapala

One of the first things you notice in towns around Lake Chapala is the number of young women between the ages of 18 and 35. You see them strolling along the cobblestone streets day and night usually in pairs. You almost never see a woman walking with a man.

Why is this? Many of the men leave home at around age 18 to go to the U.S. or Canada in search of higher wages. Some tiny villages in Mexico have virtually no young men at all.

The powerful lure toward higher wages in the north is easy to understand. A typical hourly wage around Lake Chapala is 50 cents compared to maybe $5.00 an hour or more in the U.S. or Canada.

The main force driving these young men toward more money is the thought of sending money back home to boost the family living standard. Just imagine what an extra $50 a week could mean to a large family getting by on $5.00 a week.

Back to the women. You will be stunned at how attractive they are. You won't see any walking around in jeans or slacks. Instead, most wear colorful, short dresses and skirts with high heel shoes.

For some reason I have always believed Mexican

women were short and a little chunky with wide facial features. Not so. Most women are tall and slim with American-looking features. Their pitch black hair, white teeth and tanned skin makes these women among the most attractive in the world.

Some say Mexican women make very good wives. They are hard-working, affectionate and have low expectations for material things. One American married to a Mexican gal said, "They won't drive you to an early grave like American women. They are satisfied with less. Don't need big houses, fancy cars, furs or jewelry."

The divorce rate in the Lake Chapala area is low by American standards. It's probably less that 1%. The influence of the church, the uncomplicated way of life and the low expectations of marriage account for the low incidence of divorce.

While divorce is not a problem, teenage pregnancy is. When this happens the baby is assimilated into the family and the mother becomes an "Aunt". The church influence works against teen pregnancies. But when so many boyfriends are leaving the tiny villages around Lake Chapala in search of better wages it is understandable why it happens. Many girls don't even tell boyfriends working in big cities about their pregnancies. Maybe that is why so many teenage mothers become "Aunts".

Prejudice

The Mexican people around Lake Chapala do not show prejudice toward blacks or other U.S. minorities.

Among the permanent American residents over the years have been many black Americans and Jews. They are treated warmly by the Mexican people as are all Americans.

"Mexican people don't even notice someone is black here in Lake Chapala," one black American told us. "Skin color or heritage has no particular significance to these simple people."

The Orphanage Of Lake Chapala

The Mexican government does not support any type of welfare or public assistance programs. So what happens to orphans who have no parents? What about neglected kids who are victims of child abuse? Who cares for them? Someone bigger than the biggest government bureaucracy: The Padre.

The Padre is a giant strapping man, broad shouldered with a long lean waistline. He himself is an orphan from Mexico City with no idea of who his parents are.

Fully understanding the burdens of growing up without a mother or father, the Padre has devoted his life to caring for orphan children. But the Padre's strong commitment could not always put food on the table. So thank heaven for the Americans living at Lake Chapala.

Several years ago Americans discovered the Padre's orphans sleeping in an abandoned building under boards leaning against a crumbling wall. "It was a sight to behold," an involved American explained. "The Padre had about 30 orphans there. At night the kids would cuddle up together to keep warm. Sometimes several little tots shared a hole-ridden blanket. But the Padre never gave up hope."

Things are much improved now for the orphans,

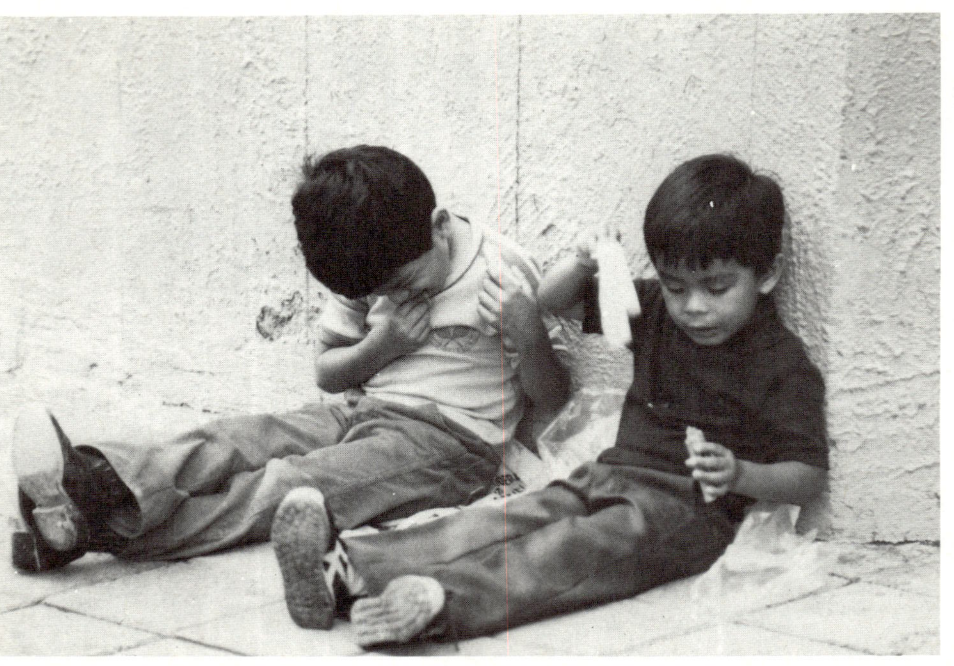

Two little boys take time out for a snack. The children are amazingly well-behaved.

thanks to the commitment of caring American residents of Lake Chapala. Over the years they have raised money through benefits and other fund raising events.

Thanks to these efforts, the Padre now has a modest farm-like complex where his orphans stay. The place is about six miles west of Ajijic right off the main road that goes around the Lake. The kids now sleep in a large clean dormatory each with his own bed and blanket. They all share the work. Some kids help cook, others clean. All the kids also attend school during the day.

Right now there are about two hundred kids living in the Padre's orphanage. The kids ages range from two to about fourteen.

The Padre refuses to turn kids away. Almost every week someone drops off another kid needing a home. Some kids have no parents. Others have been abandoned. Some are victims of abuse. The Padre takes them all in.

None of the kids are available for adoption or foster home care. Why? Because when kids are dropped off at the orphanage, the Padre never asks questions. He just takes the kids in. As a result the Padre doesn't know who "owns" the kids. He doesn't have "legal title" and can't give any kid away.

The orphanage is totally supported by donations. But the Padre's dream is to make the orphanage 100% self sufficient. The Padre hopes some day the kids will grow their own crops, raise livestock and make their own way without help. Each kid would be taught a skill. Upon leaving the orphanage, the Padre would ask each kid to come back and work a year for the benefit of the remaining orphans.

When you visit Lake Chapala, go see the orphanage and meet the Padre and his kids.

Children in Chapala are prised possessions. Mothers keep them dressed like little dolls.

Supplementing Your Income
At Lake Chapala

Everything is so cheap at Lake Chapala most Americans aren't looking to make extra money. But if you want to earn money or just dabble around in something to keep busy, there are ample opportunities for you here.

First of all, Mexican law prohibits tourists from holding a job. Only permanent residents with Immigrado status can legally work in Mexico. This is explained later. The Mexican government is sensitive to any kind of work opportunity going to a non-Mexican. I guess they figure there's hardly enough jobs to go around for Mexicans. So if you're planning any work activity on a large scale you should get the advice of a good Mexican lawyer.

Americans are making money in the Lake Chapala through:

--buying and selling real estate,

--managing property,

--finders fees, and

--renting out their cars.

Buying And Selling Real Estate

If you are interested in real estate you can try your hand at making a few bucks here. Most Americans dealing in real estate buy homes in need of repair from Mexican owners. Then they fix them up and sell to other Americans at a profit.

There is no limit on the number of properties you can "own" at one time. Many Americans concentrate on one or two properties a year in their spare time.

Homes like this right on the water can be bought for a fraction of the cost in other countries.

Some Americans reportedly make a comfortable living at Lake Chapala through real estate transactions.

Property Management

Some Americans choose to live at Lake Chapala only part of the year. The rest of the year they live in the U.S. or another country. When these Americans are not at Lake Chapala they want someone to look after their property. This creates an opportunity for other Americans looking to pick up a few dollars.

What is involved? Most people want peace of mind knowing someone is keeping an eye on things while they are gone. Others want the grass cut and the grounds kept up.

Some Americans allow their Mexican help to live-in while they're away. They do this because they don't want to lose a good maid or cook to someone else. In these situations the property manager supervises the activities of the help.

Finders Fees

Real Estate agencies at Lake Chapala charge a 20% commission to sell a home. That is a whopping fee by U.S. standards. Most U.S. real estate agencies charge about 6% commission.

Any real estate agent (or private seller) will gladly pay you a 10% finders fee if you produce a buyer for them. Because of this incentive, some Americans routinely show interested American visitors homes for sale. If the person you showed a home to eventually buys that home you get the finders fee.

This is one of the many beautiful, mountainside homes that overlook the Lake. Almost all of these homes are occupied by Americans or Canadians. Most of the People live at the Lake year-round. Others maintain a home for several months a year. Some of these homes are owned by wealthy doctors who practice medicine in Guadalajara. They use these homes for a weekend retreat.

Renting Cars

Renting a car from one of the major companies like Hertz or Avis is expensive. You will have to shell out about $40 a day or more including insurance and taxes. So a week's rental could cost you almost $300. But many Americans living at Lake Chapala will rent you their car for $100 a week or so depending on the kind of car.

Because it's cheaper to rent from an American than from a car rental company, these cars are in demand. This means extra income for the car owner. Some Americans pick up several thousand dollars a year or more renting out their cars.

Persons wanting to rent a car simply take a cab from Guadalajara Airport to Lake Chapala (A cost of about $9.00). In Chapala they call the owner who will drop off the car at a convenient location. It's a good deal for both the American car owner and the visitor.

Buying A House In Lake Chapala

Buying property in Mexico is different than in the U.S. Only a Mexican citizen can enjoy "forever ownership" in Mexico. All others own a property for a maximum of thirty years. After thirty years, the property must be sold at the market value with the full sale price going to the owner.

Your title to the property is held in trust at a Mexican bank. You can sell your property to anyone at anytime with no penalties or restrictions. If you sell to a non-Mexican, the new owner acquires the balance of your 30 year trust. Of course, if you sell to a Mexican, he gets forever ownership.

One of the many beautiful homes occupied by Americans. This home is on a hill and has a magnificent Lake view. Homes like this run about one-third the cost in the States.

The Trustee bank charges a small fee for setting up the trust. The buyer must pay for the title search, registration and other fees. Typically these costs are insignificant.

Price Range Of Homes

Whatever your financial situation, you can find a home at Lake Chapala to suit your needs. The price of homes range from about $15,000 up to $350,000.

At the lower price you're looking at a smaller home about 700 square feet or a larger home in need of repair. The higher price range will get you a mansion with 4000 or more square feet on the Lake or hillside overlooking the Lake.

Homes are probably one of the most expensive things at Lake Chapala even though they are cheap by U.S. standards. Homes anywhere in the world tend to have an international value, regardless of local living standards. That's because many of the materials used to build a home, like copper and lumber, have an international value. Only the labor to build the home is cheaper.

Terms Of Sale

Homes at Lake Chapala usually sell for cash although terms are occasionally available. Terms are more common when buying from a Mexican citizen. The price of the home is usually in U.S. dollars even when buying from a Mexican.

Real estate agencies charge owners a 20% commission to sell their home. This 20% is generally reflected in a higher home price. Therefore you generally get a better bargain when dealing direct with the owner of a home.

Not only are homes cheap, but taxes and utilities are low. Taxes and utilities on a home like this would be about $100 a year.

Styles Of Homes

Generally homes at Lake Chapala have two different types of architecture: Spanish and American style.

The Spanish style architecture is the most functional and most popular. Spanish style homes are built around a courtyard or pool. The entire property is normally walled-in for maximum privacy. Under this type of design the center of living activity is outside. With the perpetual summer climate here at Lake Chapala it's no wonder this style home is so popular.

It is interesting that Spanish-style homes are designed similar to the towns. Towns are built around a square which is the center of the town's activity.

American style homes are not built around a pool or courtyard and are not walled-in. Instead they look like homes you would find in almost any suburb in the U.S. Virtually all of these American style homes were built by non-Mexicans.

Things To Watch For
When Buying A Home

When buying a home at Lake Chapala you're not likely to have problems, especially if you deal with a real estate firm. However, there are several things you should watch out for.

An important consideration is the water supply. Most homes around the Lake get water from a well. Once in awhile these wells go dry, and a new one has to be drilled. This can be expensive and a source of inconvenience. So make sure to run all faucets and flush toilets to check out the water pressure.

Of course, you will also want to have a termite inspection. While termites are not a serious problem at

This is an American-style home in the town of Chapala between Chapala and Ajijic.

the Lake, they do exist. A simple termite test can spot potential problems.

Of course, make sure you have good title to the property. It's a good idea to hire an English-speaking Mexican lawyer to make sure all paperwork is in order. To find a lawyer, get a recommendation from one of the American residents at the Lake, or call the Lake Chapala Society.

As mentioned, you'll probably pay a little more for a home when buying through a real estate agency. But you'll also avoid problems. An agent can point out good and bad features about a home and it's location. The agent can tell you many things an anxious seller may overlook.

One last point. Lake Chapala is not for everyone. Before buying you should rent a home for at least 6 months. This will give you time to check things out thoroughly before you make a commitment to buy.

Renting A Home

Many Americans live at Lake Chapala part time. When away they rent their home to visitors. You should have no problem renting one of these homes. However, during the snowbird season--from December to February--the supply of homes to rent can dwindle because so many Americans come to Lake Chapala to get away from the blistering cold winter.

What is the going rent for a home? A rule of thumb: monthly rent should be about 5% of the home's value per month. For example if the home is worth $50,000, the rent should be about $250 a month.

Most Americans renting a home at Lake Chapala stay

An American-style home in the town of Chula Vista which is between Ajijic and Chapala. These American-style homes are not walled-in and are not built around a courtyard like the Mexican-style homes. Virtually all these American-style homes were built by non-Mexicans.

from two to six months. Generally, if you're staying less than a month you're better off staying at a hotel.

Where To Eat At Lake Chapala

The restaurants at Lake Chapala are among the finest you will find anywhere. Certainly the prices will be the lowest you have seen in a long time. I was really surprised to find such good food in these tiny towns. What's more, you won't need a reservation. And you'll probably never wait for a table.

What's the reason for the great food here? Many of the restaurants are owned or managed by Americans or Canadians. Most operated successful restaurants in large cities but left for the slower pace of life at Lake Chapala.

The most popular (and the best) restaurants at Lake Chapala are the La Viuda, Posada and Real de Chapala.

La Viude

The La Viude is located in the heart of Chapala around the corner from the Hotel Nido.

The food and service are excellent. This is the most popular restaurant in the area. You can eat inside or outside in a tropical courtyard. The La Viuda offers a great salad bar as good as any I've seen in the states.

You can see entire menu at the back of the book.

Anything is good, but my favorite is the broiled red snapper. You get a complete, generous-sized fish that's excellent. It comes with your choice of potatoes and vegetables plus all you want from the salad bar.

The chateaubriand is a big favorite. Some say you can't find better no matter where you go.

The La Viuda is owned by Gus, who also owns the butcher shop next door where most Americans buy their meats.

The Posada

The Posada is located in Ajijic on the Lake. The Posada is the main "hang out" for Americans living around the Lake. Any time day or night you'll find Americans here drinking, eating and socializing.

Every night the Posada has a different dinner special. A favorite of many Americans is the American-style spaghetti. It's very good and comes with salad, vegetables, bread and butter. The price is about $2.75 for the complete meal. You can see the entire menu at the back of the book.

The Posada is owned by a Canadian couple who have plenty of restaurant experience. They know how to prepare food that pleases Americans and Canadians. That's why this place is so popular.

Real de Chapala

The Real de Chapala is located just east of Ajijic. It's on the Lake about a half mile off the main road that goes around the Lake.

The Real de Chapala is owned and operated by the University of Guadalajara. Prominent medical doctors from Guadalajara visit and dine here regularly. Is the food good here? You bet. You can see the entire menu at the back of the book.

Everything is good, but my favorite is the barbequed chicken. You can eat in the enclosed dining room or in the outside garden area by the pool.

Every Sunday the Real de Chapala hosts an old fashioned Mexican-style buffet. They serve a wide

This is the famous restaurant and bar frequented by Americans and Canadians. The Posada has nice hotel rooms, restaurant and bar. They have entertainment twice a week. This is the most popular place to go at Lake Chapala if you are a non-Mexican.

variety of Mexican dishes right outside in the tropical garden. You can enjoy "Old-Mexico" mariachi music and authentic Mexican food. It's a great way to spend Sunday afternoon. Try it, you'll love it.

Other Good Restaurants

Other less fancy, but good restaurants--especially for breakfast and lunch--are the Cafe de Paris and the Superior. Both are located on the main street of Chapala. These are popular American spots. The food is great and the prices are especially low. At both restarurants you can sit for hours and watch people walking by.

The Cafe de Paris and Superior are noted for their fish and vegetable chowders and soups. You can get a good meal at either restaurant for under $2.

Feeling at Home

The thought of being in a foreign country thousands of miles from home instills fear in some people. The "what if" syndrome takes over their thinking. "What if I need help. What if I get sick. What if. What if."

No one will say living at Lake Chapala is the same as living in the U.S., but you won't be as isolated as you may think.

First of all, there are an estimated 30,000 Americans living in Guadalajara, less than 30 miles from Lake Chapala. Over the years these Americans have brought pieces of the U.S. to Mexico, making life more comfortable.

Most things you'll need are available at the Lake or

This is the main road that goes around Lake Chapala. The part shown here goes through Ajijic. The roads are surprisingly wide and well-maintained.

A view of the Lake from the Monte Carlo country club just outside the town of Chapala. Many Americans belong to this club. It is also open to the public.

The Monte Carlo Club on a gloomy day. The Monte Carlo is owned by the University of Guadalajara. It fronts the Lake and has magnificent grounds. The club has a number of motel rooms and
several restaurants. It is probably the most popular place to stay other than the Hotel Real de
Chapala.

Guadalajara. Here is a partial list of things available that will make you feel more at home.

The Lake Chapala Society

Since 1955 the Lake Chapala Society has helped Americans and Canadians settle at the Lake. Located in Ajijic, the Society is staffed by volunteers who can give information and advice to newcomers to the area. The Society staff can help you find a place to stay for a few months or forever. The staff can help you locate a maid, gardener or cook. They can also introduce you to other Americans and Canadians living around the Lake.

The Society's building has a large bulletin board which posts articles for sale and lists coming events and other information of importance to English speaking residents.

The Society publishes a monthly bulletin and holds a luncheon once a month for its members.

English Newspapers

There are two main English newspapers: the "Colony Reporter" and "The Mexico City News."

The Colony Reporter gives news of interest to Americans living in Guadalajara and Lake Chapala. It covers everything affecting Americans from what to do to local problems. A large classified section covers real estate and automobiles for sale, houses and apartments for rent, and personal matters.

The News comes out every day and covers international news with emphasis on the U.S. and Mexico. The News is a comprehensive, quality paper as good as any daily.

Lake Chapala has its own English Library located in

This is the Lake Chapala Society Building. Here you can get a variety of American books and periodicals. You can also get assistance on housing and domestic help matters.

Ajijic. Some Guadalajara libraries have English-written books.

Shopping

Lake Chapala has several supermarkets that stock most products available in America. Of course most everything is cheaper except certain canned goods imported from the U.S.

Most Americans living at the Lake make monthly runs to Guadalajara to do their "heavy shopping." Guadalajara has several giant American-style shopping centers. The most popular is Plaza del sol. It's the most modern shopping center in Latin America.

When shopping, don't overlook the thousands of small independently-owned shops. Mexico has a wider variety of hand-crafted items than anywhere in the world. You will find a huge selection of hand crafted stone, gold, silver, copper, iron, bronze, as well as glass, clay, leather, wool and cotton.

Medical Care

In Mexico, a pharmacist plays a greater role in health care than in the U.S. Many medicines that require a doctor's prescription in the U.S. are available "over the counter" at drugstores in Mexico. Many Americans living at the Lake let the pharmacist handle most of their medical needs. For example, minor ailments such as colds, sore throats and stomach discomforts can almost always be taken care of with something prescribed by the Chapala Pharmacist.

For serious ailments most Americans visit the American/Mexican Medical Center in Guadalajara. The quality of health care is reported to be as good as a U.S. facility. Of course, for complicated surgery like a heart bypass or organ transplant you're better off going to a U.S. medical facility.

For persons worried about major medical problems, there is an insurance plan available in Guadalajara that will handle air transportation (and in-flight emergency care) to any hospital in the U.S. The cost is small and the quality of service is reportedly good.

Many American doctors have received their training at the University of Guadalajara medical school. This modern medical school has trained U.S. students unable to get into a U.S. medical school because of enrollment limitations. When these American students graduate, they can receive the same accreditation as a U.S. graduated student.

Schools

It's a little embarrassing when Mexican kids eight or nine years old blurt out fluent English when most Americans can barely recite a sentence in Spanish without stumbling. This is a credit to the outstanding schools in Guadalajara. Three years of English is required in the Mexican school system. It's surprising that about 15% of the school kids (five to eighteen years old) in Guadalajara are American. These are the children of families with resident (Immigrado) status.

Many Americans--some former teachers themselves--believe the schools in Guadalajara are first rate.

The Library

A library with books and periodicals in English is located in Ajijic (16 de Septembre 16A). This library is open daily (except Sundays and holidays) from 10 a.m. to 1 p.m. The library is staffed by volunteers who can answer questions about the Lake Chapala area.

A view of the Lake from the Monte Carlo country club.

For a larger selection of English language books you can visit the Benjamin Franklin Library located in the American Consulate in Guadalajara. This library is open to the general public. Books can be signed out with a library card.

Sunday -- Day of Celebration

Monday through Saturday the tiny town of Chapala is quiet. People work hard all day then spend time at home with the family at night. But come Sunday the town explodes into a full blown celebration.

"Excuse me, is today a Mexican holiday?" Dad said to a passerby in Chapala.

"Oh no," said the stranger, "This is just a normal Sunday. It's sort of like a Saturday night in the States. The town's people celebrate the week gone by. It's a family affair. Everyone participates from the youngest tot to the oldest granny."

Sure enough Chapala had come alive. It looked like the 4th of July. The "boardwalk" next to the Lake was crowded with people of all ages. It was a great night to be outdoors. The temperature was perfect with a refreshing breeze blowing in from the Lake. It was relaxing. You could hear the mariachi bands playing "Old-Mexico" style music. Street vendors were everywhere peddling white roasted corn, fresh fruit, nuts and hot pastries.

After walking awhile, Dad and I sat on a bench overlooking the Lake and boardwalk. On the Lake shore is a large outside bar and dance hall called the "Beergarden." In the Beergarden we could see people dancing and having a good time.

This is an early morning view of the beergarden. Here you can get food and drink and sit alongside the Lake. On Sunday night the beergarden explodes into activity. They have at least one or two bands that play late into the night. Sunday is the biggest night at Lake Chapala. Everyone works hard during the week, looking forward to a good time on Sunday. Everyone in the family participates, even the children.

"Let's walk over to the beergarden--looks like fun over there," I said to Dad.

It was a real family outing, like an old fashioned Polish wedding. You could see older folks on the dance floor kicking up their heels. Right next to them were little tots holding hands and skipping around the dance floor. Even the band members were having a good time. They played some of the liveliest toe-tapping music I've heard in awhile. They played for over two hours at a time without a break.

This night was a nice experience. I especially enjoyed the great music and fun-loving people. When it was finally over I couldn't wait until next Sunday so I could do it all over again.

Getting To Paradise

The great thing about Lake Chapala is that it's not far from home no matter where you live in North America. For example, from Detroit or Chicago you're only about five hours away by air. From San Diego or Los Angeles it's only two and a half hours away. Even when driving you are only a few days away from most cities in the United States.

Driving to Lake Chapala

Many Americans drive to Lake Chapala and Guadalajara each year with no trouble whatsoever. But before you start on your drive to Lake Chapala there are a few precautions you should take.

The east end of Lake Chapala on a gloomy day.

An early morning view of the walkway along the Lake in Chapala. To the right is the beautiful Chapala park. To the left is the pier where tiny fishing boats go off to fish each morning.

Before Leaving

Before leaving, have your car checked for potential problems. Routine maintenance items such as tires, hoses and fan belts should be replaced if needed. Make sure nothing goes wrong. That's easier than trying to fix something once it breaks down.

You'll need Mexican auto insurance before you cross the border. Most U.S. auto insurance policies do not cover driving in Mexico. You can ask your regular agent about coverage or buy it at any border town. It is a good idea to get comprehensive coverage.

Some Americans have been involved in auto accidents in Mexico only to find their U.S. policies didn't cover them. This can be a real pain in the neck. You can be held in a Mexican jail until you demonstrate you are able to pay for all damages. If the accident was serious, you could be looking at extensive medical bills and personal liability. The Mexican system of justice is sometimes based on the Napoleonic code. That is, "guilty until proven inocent."

All problems can be avoided simply by purchasing Mexican insurance. It's simple to buy and it's relatively inexpensive. If you are involved in an accident simply produce your policy to the police. In all probability you won't be detained.

Your U.S. drivers license is valid in Mexico. You won't need any special permit to operate your vehicle.

Of course, be sure you have proof of car ownership. If you plan to drive a leased or borrowed car, you'll need a notarized statement of permission to drive the car.

Lastly, have your trip mapped out before you leave. See your insurance agent about the best route from your particular area. Be sure you find out about any detours and ongoing road repairs.

An inside view of the Nido Hotel. This hotel was built about 100 years ago. It is one of the cleanest hotels in Mexico. The rooms are modest and start at about $5 a night. The food at the Nido is good. Prices are very reasonable. This restaurant is very popular with Americans. The Nido is located in the heart of the town of Chapala.

At the Border

At the border you must get a permit for your car. The permit is generally issued for the same period as your visitors card, up to a maximum of 180 days. If you expect to return to the border more than once before your permit expires, you should request a multiple entry permit. Otherwise a single entry permit will do.

When you drive your car to Mexico you must take it with you when you leave. This is to prevent the car from being sold in Mexico. The import tax on automobiles in Mexico is very high. Someone could make a fortune bringing cars into Mexico, avoiding the import tax, and selling at the market value. That's why the Mexican government has established its policy of requiring cars to stay with the owners when crossing the border.

What happens if you have to leave Mexico in an emergency? Most people post a bond with the Mexican immigration office. This provides assurance that the car will eventually be returned to the U.S. and not sold in Mexico.

Trailers

Thanks to a recent law mobile homes can be left in a registered trailer park when the owner crosses the border. This new law is a real blessing to thousands of Americans and Canadians who have mobile homes in Mexico.

Driving in Mexico

Your drive to Lake Chapala should be pleasurable and exciting. Thousands of Americans drive throughout Mexico each year without problems of any kind.

On your way to Lake Chapala it's a good idea not to

It is not unusual to see donkeys strolling down the cobblestone streets in the towns around the Lake. The animals co-exist nicely with the cars.

drive at night. This is common sense. If you experience car trouble it's more difficult to get help at night than during daylight hours. What's more, when driving at night through farming areas, livestock crossing a road is hard to see. By the way, if you hit a farm animal, the owner is liable for all damages to your car. The only problem is you might have trouble tracking down the owner.

Getting gas for your car in Mexico is no problem. The Mexican government owns all of the gas stations. These government operated stations are called Pemex. They sell leaded and non-leaded fuel. Pemex prices are about half what you pay in the U.S. The Pemex stations don't accept credit cards of any kind, so have pesos handy.

Throughout Mexico, government employees called Green Angels, patrol the major highways to help motorists. These Green Angels patrol in green trucks between 8:00 a.m. and 9:00 p.m. every day except Tuesday. On Tuesday they start patrolling at noon. Most Green Angels speak English. They can help with minor repairs or give you an emergency supply of gasoline. The Green Angels don't charge for their service. You pay only for parts or gas or oil used.

If you have car trouble, pull off the road and raise your hood. Wait for help to come.

If your car needs major repair Mexican mechanics are familiar with most American and foreign makes. The Green Angeles can help you find a competent mechanic.

Road Signs

Most road signs in Mexico are "international" and don't require a knowledge of Spanish to figure out. Other important road signs are posted in Spanish. Obviously it's a good idea to know what they mean.

Below you'll find a listing of the principle Mexican
and international road signs.

Doble Circulacion
Two Way Traffic

Glorieta
Rotary Intersection

Transicion
Transition

Tramo Angosto
Road Narrows

Puente Angosto
Narrow Bridge

Altura Maxima
Vertical Clearance (m)

Camino Derrapante
Slippery Road

Pendiente
Hill

Vado
Dip

Cruce Ferrocarriles
Railroad Crossing

Trabajadores
Workmen

Escuela
School Zone

Zona de Derrumbes
Slide Area
(Watch for Falling Rocks)

Semaforo
Traffic Light

Ganado
Cattle

Stop

Yield
Right of Way

Inspection

Speed Limit
(km)

One Way
Traffic

No
Pedestrians

Keep
Right

No
U Turn

Horizontal
Clearance (m)

No Left Turn

Do Not Pass

Do Not Enter

One Hour
Parking

Parking Limit

No Parking

The Mexican people are happy and fun-loving. They cherish the celebration of life.

Traveling On Mexican Holidays

While on the road during a Mexican holiday you're likely to find some businesses closed. This means services you may need will be unavailable. So it's a good idea to avoid traveling in remote areas on holidays. Mexican National Holidays are listed below.

Date	Commemorating
January 1	New Year's Day
February 5	Constitution Day
February 24	Flag Day
March 21	Birthday of Benito Juarez
(date varies)	Easter
May 1	Labor Day
May 5	Battle of Puebla
May 10	Mother's Day
September 1	President's State of the Union Message
September 16	Independence Day
October 12	*Dia de la Raza* (Columbus Day)
November 20	Revolution Day
December 25	Christmas

Distance to Lake Chapala

Lake Chapala is only a few day's drive from most cities in the United States. For example, from New York City Lake Chapala is only about 2,675 miles. That's about 100 miles less than a trip from New York to Los Angeles.

Below is a map showing distances to Lake Chapala from key cities in the U.S.

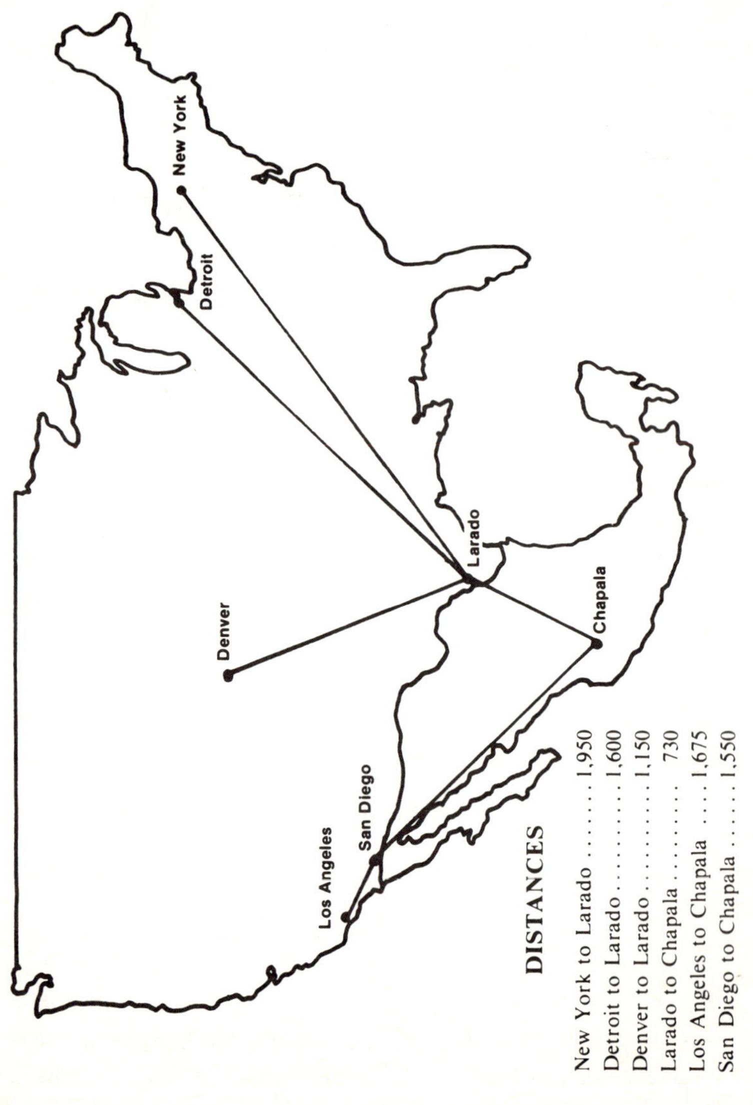

Crossing The Border
Immigration Requirements

Before entering Mexico on your way to Lake Chapala you'll need a Mexican tourist card. This tourist card is easy to get and it's free.

The tourist cards are available at the border crossing, or you can get one from your travel agent or airline. Before being issued a tourist card you'll have to demonstrate you're an American (or Canadian) citizen. A passport, birth certificate, voting card, or naturalization papers are all you'll need.

The tourist card allows you to be in Mexico for up to 180 days. But sometimes the Immigration Officer at the border will try to stamp your tourist card for less than 180 days. So if you plan to stay in Mexico for several months, let the Immigration Officer know it's important to stamp 180 days on your card.

The Immigration Officer has a great deal of flexibility in deciding how many days to stamp on your card. Some people say the Immigration Officer places a lot of emphasis on how you and your party look. So in requesting the full 180 days try to be courteous and insistant at the same time. Some Americans give the Immigration Officer a "tip" for stamping the full 180 days on their tourist card.

If your tourist card is stamped less than 180 days, you can have it extended to the full 180 days while in Mexico. The usual procedure is to visit the Mexican Immigration Office in Guadalajara about ten days before your card is about to expire. You can generally get an automatic extension.

Of course if you are visiting a border town in Mexico like Tijuana or Juarez you don't need a tourist card.

A view down a cobblestone street in the town of Ajijic. In most towns around the Lake you get a magnificent view of either the mountains or the Lake.

You only need a card for trips deeper into Mexico.

What happens when your tourist card expires, but you want to stay at Lake Chapala longer? You will have to return to the U.S., re-enter Mexico and get a new tourist card. This procedure is not as bad as it sounds. Most Americans and Canadians living at Lake Chapala plan visits to family or shopping around required "immigration runs."

Retiree Visitor Card - F.M. 2 Permit

You can apply for a Retiree Visitor Card at any Mexican Consulate in the U.S. (or Canada). This card allows you to live in Mexico as a retiree for 6 months at a time. The Card is renewable in Mexico 4 times for a maximum of 24 months. This method eliminates the necessity of returning to the border and re-entering Mexico every 6 months.

Resident Immigrant Status - F.M. 3 Permit

You can apply for Permanent Resident (Immigrado) status at any Mexican Consulate in the U.S. (or Canada) or the Immigration Office in Mexico City. The permit can be issued to any foreigner meeting certain requirements and having a permanent income (from a pension or bank deposit or other sources) sufficient to live in Mexico. This permit is issued on a temporary basis but becomes permanent after five years. The permit must be renewed annually for the first 5 years. After that a Permanent Immigrant status is granted.

Immigrado status gives you nearly all of the rights and privileges of a Mexican Citizen. You can operate a business, hold a job and own property. An experienced English-speaking lawyer should handle your paper work when applying for this status.

What You Can Legally Bring Into Mexico

Most people planning to stay in Mexico bring some of their possessions with them. Before bringing personal items into Mexico you should know customs restrictions.

Listed below are some examples of what you can bring into Mexico:

- Up to 50 cigars, 200 cigarettes, or 250 grams of tobacco.
- Up to 50 books, as long as none are pornographic (Penthouse and Playboy magazines are considered pornographic in Mexico).
- One regular camera and one movie camera, with 12 rolls of film each.
- Used sporting equipment, except for spearfishing equipment (spearfishing is illegal in Mexico). Guns are subject to special restrictions.
- Tools and professional equipment as long as you don't plan to set up shop in Mexico.
- Used children's toys.
- Up to five gifts.
- Electrical appliances, including radios and televisions.
- No fruits, flowers or plants.
- Pets may enter Mexico only with a certificate of

An early morning view of the pier at Chapala. The fishing boats at the right can take you out to a nearby island. The boats will also take you on a tour of the Lake. The prices are very reasonable.

good health signed by a veterinarian, and a certificate of rabies vaccination, dated within the last six months.

Check with Mexican Customs Officials for complete information on customs restrictions.

Changing Dollars Into Pesos

The peso's rate of exchange is generally unstable and often difficult to predict. The value of the peso is closely tied to the Mexican rate of inflation, oil prices and other economic and political considerations. Therefore, it is a good idea to exchange your dollars to pesos on an "as needed" basis. This is important to remember in order to maximize your dollar's purchasing power.

It's better to exchange dollars to pesos at one of Mexico's National Banks. The rate will be posted in the front window. The exchange rate is the same at all banks so don't bother shopping around. All banks in Mexico are owned and operated by the government. Banks are open Monday through Friday, 9 a.m. to 1:30 p.m. Some branches are open Saturday mornings.

Dealing with a bank is more predictable than relying on merchants to give you the going rate of exchange. It's not that local merchants would intentionally cheat you. It's just that the peso's value is in a continual state of change--decline is a better word--and all merchants do not keep up with its day-to-day value.

The permanent American residents at the Lake generally keep their money in a U.S. money market account with check-writing privileges. They get a steady income and their money is safe. When pesos are needed they simply write a check on their account and cash it at

98

a local Mexican bank where they have an account.

Some American residents keep substantial amounts of money in local Mexican banks. Why? Let's assume a peso account pays about 48 percent annual interest, paid monthly. You can live off the interest on a $10,000 investment.

Here is how it works. Let's say you convert $10,000 dollars to Mexican pesos and deposit that sum in a 2-year certificate of deposit paying 48% interest a year. This means you earn pesos equal to about $5,000 a year, or about $100 a week. On that amount you can live comfortably at Lake Chapala. That is the good news.

The bad news is the peso is probably loosing value every day. Let's say it's losing value at a rate of 17 centavos per day (17% of a peso. A peso is worth 100 centavos). At that rate your original $10,000 investment would be worth about $5,000 after two years. But wait! The bottom line is that you have lived comfortably at Lake Chapala for a full two years and it cost you only about $5,000. That is why many Americans living at the Lake keep a good deal of money in a peso account at a Mexican bank.

Mailing Letters and Postcards
From Mexico

When mailing a letter or post card out of Mexico be sure to use Mexican stamps only. If you use U.S. stamps the Mexican Post Office will not deliver it and they won't even return it to you.

Go to a local post office to find out how much postage you need. Post offices are usually open from 9 a.m. to 7 p.m., Monday through Friday. Or Saturday hours are usually 9 a.m. to 5 p.m.

Out Of The Rat Race

It was early Sunday morning. I was sitting at the town square in Ajijic. The sun was just starting to take the chill off. The temperature a pleasant 65 degrees. You could feel a nice breeze coming in off the Lake. Not bad, considering the temperature in Detrot was around zero. I was relaxed. Just enjoying the scenery. Kids playing. A dog or two lounging around. Older people sitting quietly.

Suddenly, a woman about 50 sat next to me. She had dark hair--streaked with gray. She had a very youthful-looking figure. A nice smile. White teeth. She said nothing for a moment or two.

Finally she said, "You must be new here in the Lake Chapala area?"

"Yes, my father and I recently arrived. Just enjoying a little vacation," I replied.

"I've been here for about 3½ years now. I basically came here on a weekend trip and never went back," she explained.

"Never went back where?" I questioned.

"San Francisco. Came here with a girlfriend. Stayed 3 or 4 days. Fell in love with the place. Never went back," she continued.

"How about friends. Don't you visit the U.S. from time to time?" I probed.

"I go back for requried border runs--to renew my visa. Other than that I have no desire to go back."

"How about family?" I asked.

One of the many picturesque views of streets that lead down to the Lake. The cobblestone streets, the green trees and the Lake in the background make this one of the prettiest areas in the world.

"I've never been married. My mother died when I was a young girl. My dad died at 65 several years ago. I have no close family in California or any place else," she explained.

She went on to say she lives right on the Lake in a Spanish-style home she bought shortly after moving here. She has a housekeeper and cook named Maria. In San Francisco she was a successful medical doctor specializing in gynecology. For several years she headed the surgical unit at a major hospital.

It was hard for me to believe that based on a single weekend trip a highly successful medical doctor would leave everything in California and come here to live, so I probed further.

"Do you practice medicine in the Lake Chapala area?" I questioned.

"I'm not licensed to practice in Mexico. Even if I could get a license I would not practice. I gave it up 3 years ago. I occasionally give medical advice to close friends who live in the area."

"On occasion I consult with local Mexican doctors. I only give advice on medical techniques. I don't get involved in the actual surgery. I just watch and monitor procedures."

As we sat chatting I noticed it was 10:30 already. I had to meet Dad. He was shopping at the Chapala market. I explained how I was enjoying the conversation but I had to meet my father.

"Why don't you and your father come for dinner tonight?" she suggested.

"Sounds great to me," I answered.

"How about 6 o'clock?"

"Great," I replied.

She stood up and pointed directly behind me, "You

View of the lakeside park in Chapala. This beautiful park has several different kinds of pretty flowers and plants. There are benches where you can sit and look out at the Lake. The park is never crowded.

walk straight down that cobblestone street. When you get to the end, it's the last house. Right on the Lake. I'll be waiting for you and your dad at 6 o'clock. We'll talk further," she instructed.

"We'll be there," I responded.

Dad was happy when I told him about dinner. When 6 o'clock rolled along we hopped in our Volkswagen and drove to Ajijic.

When we arrived at her home we saw a cobblestone wall with a door in the center. The home appeared modest. Dad and I walked up to the house. The Doctor was standing there waiting for us.

"Hi fellas, I've been expecting you. Come in," she insisted.

At that moment it dawned on me. The Doctor and I had talked at length this morning but overlooked exchanging names.

"This is my father, Al. My name is Roger," I said.

"Helen Little is my name. Friends call me Doc," she said with a wide smile. "Come in. Sit in the living room. I have a few things to do. I'll have Maria make you comfortable."

Dad and I could not believe the spaciousness and beauty of the place. The home was approximately four to five thousand square feet. It was gorgeous. The home was built around a large swimming pool--right at the foot of the Lake. You had the option of enjoying the pool or walking 30 feet or so to the Lake.

The structure was 2 stories. It looked like you had a Lake view from almost any room. The front of the home was nearly all windows. On the walls were beautiful Mexican paintings and nic nacs. There was a definate Spanish flavor to the interior design. A stereo was playing soft, Mexican music.

104

Inside the restaurant El Meson. The El Meson is one of the most popular restaurants with Americans and Canadians. It serves a variety of both American and Mexican food. The service is excellent and the prices are very reasonable. You'll like this restaurant.

Dad and I looked at each other. "Who would think something like this was behind that cobblestone wall?" I said.

As we sat gazing out at the Lake, a Spanish girl about 25 approached and said, "Senors, my name is Maria. Would you like something to drink? We have beer, wine, mixed drinks, whatever you want."

"Tecate beer," I said.

"Si," she nodded.

Dad had plain orange juice.

As the maid walked back to the kitchen the Doctor walked into the living room and began talking about the house.

"I bought the home soon after coming here from San Francisco, Technically, I don't own the home--I'm leasing it for 25 years. After 25 years I'll probably be dead. So what's the difference. The house cost $90,000 3½ years ago. That was a lot of money at the time. But I recently turned down $175,000 for the home. I just couldn't sell it. The beautiful Lake view, the pool and cool breezes are hard to part with--no matter what the price. Besides, after 25 years I'll be able to sell at fair market value. Or maybe the Mexican government will renew the lease. Who knows. Whatever happens I feel I've gotten my money's worth," she explained.

She told us the home was approximately 4,650 square feet. That did not include 800 square feet in the garage. There was about 3,000 square feet downstairs and 1,650 up.

"The home is totally furnished with local crafts. The furniture and paintings were obtained in the Lake area. A few things like the couch and lamps came from Guadalajara," she said.

She told us the furniture was situated so every chair

A view of the town of Chapala. The steeples of the Church stand prominantly above the skyline.

had a view of the Lake.

"Even the kitchen and bedrooms have Lake views," she said.

As she was describing the home, Maria served our drinks. The Doctor drank a marguerita. I felt this would be a great opportunity to get further information about life here at Lake Chapala. Since the Doctor had been here 3½ years, I was sure she could fill us in on many good and bad points about the area.

Dad asked how she enjoyed her years at Lake Chapala.

"The last 3½ years have been happier than any other time in my life," she said.

"What's a typical day like here?" I questioned.

"Every morning I get up at about 5:30. The maid cooks a nutritious breakfast--usually oatmeal and fresh juice. Then I go by the pool for about 20 minutes and let the sun warm me up a little. At about 7 o'clock I put on my jogging outfit and jog about 2 miles up and down the lakeshore. After jogging I normally walk to the town square and sit awhile. There I typically have a conversation with one of the local residents or just read the paper. Then I walk to one of the local restaurants for coffee. I don't usually have coffee before 9 o'clock--after I have food in my stomach. By 10 o'clock I usually drive down to the open-air market in Chapala. I do shopping for a day or two. Shopping at the market usually takes an hour or two. Sometimes I sit at the market and have fresh juice. I can get fresh carrot juice, apple juice, grapefruit or orange juice. I'll just sit there for 15 or 20 minutes--watching people shop. Just relaxing. Once in a while I'll shop for other goods. There are all kinds of leather products and clothing available at very low prices. Almost every day I run into somebody. We'll sit,

This tree grows in the center of the Monte Carlo country club grounds. It is over 150 years old.

have a drink and chat. I'm usually finished shopping and visiting by 11:30. By then Maria's preparing lunch. This gives me a chance to sit by the pool and do a little reading. I do extensive reading, but I refuse to read any kind of medical literature. I've blocked out that part of my life completely."

"It usually takes Maria about an hour or two to prepare lunch. I normally eat at 1 or 2 o'clock. I usually have something light like a bowl of soup, fresh bread and a fruit salad. At about 3 o'clock I take my daily swim in the pool. I do at least 50 or 60 laps every day. The pool laps and jogging pretty much keep me in shape. After swimming and relaxing by the pool, it's normally about 5:30--time to get ready for dinner. I usually have Maria cook something light. More typically, I'll eat at one of the great restaurants in the area," she explained.

"Which restaurants do you normally go to?" I asked.

"My favorite restaurant is the La Viuda in Chapala. I go there about 3 times a week. The food is so cheap--it seems foolish to eat at home. I go to the Posada once or twice a week. Many Americans and Canadians go there. I also love the La Meson. They serve great Mexican food. This is another local favorite. Another favorite is the Hotel de Chapala. I go there on Sunday for the Mexican brunch. After dinner I'll go to the Posada for an after dinner drink."

"After leaving the Posada, I often walk to the town square. I'll sit there for a half hour or so before going home for the evening. That is a typical routine," she said.

"Weekends are a completely different story. On almost any Friday or Saturday night some kind of function is going on around the Lake. Typically,

Right near the town square in Chapala a dog lives on the roof. The dog barks at people walking by all day. The dog never seems to stop enjoying this.

somebody has a party. Everyone brings something. It's a nice get-together. The Lake Chapala Society, the Elks or the American Legion also hold functions. It's normally a banquet. We have a keynote speaker then dance or party afterward."

"People at Lake Chapala are very friendly. Americans, Canadians and the local Mexican people are all warm."

"What do you like most about Chapala?" Dad questioned.

"The simplicity of life," she replied. "Life in San Francisco got too complex. The bureaucracy at the hospital, legal problems, long working hours and constant stress. The pace was just too fast."

"The congestion and the traffic was also hard to deal with. Getting to work sometimes took an hour. Home was less than 10 miles away."

"Here in Lake Chapala, everything is the opposite. In California things are complex. In Lake Chapala life is uncomplicated. In California things are expensive. In Chapala prices are dirt cheap. In California it's crowded and congested. Here in Lake Chapala there is no congestion. California has a lot of pollution. Here in Chapala there is no pollution. California has high crime. Chapala has almost no crime."

I asked her if she ever yearns to go back to her medical practice in California.

"Never," she replied.

"Why would a successful medical doctor leave San Francisco for Lake Chapala?" I questioned.

Without hesitating she said, "The hipocracy of a medical establishment and the ridiculous problems with malpractice insurance."

She continued with an incredible story.

The Monte Carlo country club. The grounds here are magnificent. They include large palm trees, green shrubs and beautiful flowers of all colors. The lawn is kept up like a golf course.

"I got out of medical school in the 50's. I was an idealistic doctor who wanted to help people. I was not interested in making a lot of money. Just enough to be comfortable. I planned to open a practice in a small town. But I soon learned you had to work at a large hospital to develop skills. When I was offered a position at a hospital in San Francisco, I took it."

"The first 15 years of practice was very satisfying. I moved up to head the surgical department. In 1975 I decided to quit and open a practice in a small town north of San Francisco. I figured I could maintain a practice and keep an affiliation with the hospital."

"I decided my practice would treat poor families. I wanted to do something for those most needing medical assistance."

"At first, I worked 7 days a week--15 hours a day. After the first year I cut back to 6 days a week--12 hours a day. I treated poor people. Of my total patients, probably 75% were on government assistance. About 25% I treated free or got partial payment."

"Then I got hit with the first medical malpractice suit. One of the patients sued me. I had performed an abortion--she had a tubal pregnancy. After the operation the woman complained of pain. Her lawyer claimed the operation was not done properly. At that time my malpractice insurance was about $20,000 a year. With the malpractice suit my insurance doubled to $40,000 a year."

"The sad thing is there was no basis for the suit."

"My lawyer told me about 75% of all malpractice suits are filed by welfare recipients. These people are poor. When problems arise they contact a lawyer. Lawyers can always find some basis for a suit. The lawyer presses for a settlement. Then to avoid a costly trial, the

You can see wild horses all around Lake Chapala. These horses live in a vacant lot in a residential area near the Hotel Real de Chapala. This group of horses includes one stud and four mares. Nobody owns the horses. They just live wild by the Lake.

insurance company pays off. A long trial might cost $100,000, $200,000 or more. Paying off is usually less. This happens all the time even though a suit is absolutely baseless."

"The problem is that lawyers take cases on a contingency fee basis. This means the lawyer is not paid anything unless there is a judgment. If there is a judgment, the lawyer gets from 30%-50% of the settlement."

"The victim in all this is the doctor. For every malpractice suit filed, insurance goes up. In all I had 5 malpractice suits filed against me. All the patients were on welfare or some other federal assistance program. All those suing were represented by contingency-fee lawyers."

"Four of the five suits were settled out of court by my insurance company. One case was so ridiculous my insurance company decided to go to trial. Since we settled 4 baseless suits out of court, the word probably got around that I was an easy target. To avoid further baseless suits the insurance company decided to stand fast on this one case."

"The case was in constant litigation for 3 years. I gave depositions many times. I answered thousands of written questions--called interrogatories. All this affected my happiness. It added stress to my life."

"When the suit finally came to trial I spent 23 working days in court. I literally closed my practice down. I cancelled appointments. Referred patients to other doctors. I handled emergency cases at night."

"Finally the jury rendered a not guilty verdict. The plaintiff asked for $2.5 million. But the jury did not award a cent."

"To celebrate the end of the trial, I came here to Lake

A view of huge palm trees at the Monte Carlo country club. Some of these trees are 100 feet high.

Chapala for a 3-day trip with a friend. After 2 days I decided this kind of life was for me. A few weeks later, I went back to San Francisco, shut everything down and moved to Chapala. I've never gone back."

Dad asked how it was possible for a doctor to make money after paying $40,000 a year for insurance.

The Doctor grinned saying, "When a doctor has to pay $50, $60, $70 thousand or more for malpractice insurance it must be made up. A doctor would make maybe $60,000 a year from a typical practice. This would just cover malpractice insurance."

"To survive, many doctors are forced into "drumming up" business. This means unnecessary surgery, unnecessary procedures and unnecessary testing. Most doctors can justify this. The more tests performed, the more diagnostics done--the less chance of being hit with a malpractice suit."

"A medical practice involves a lot of hustle just to survive. That's why I like it here at Lake Chapala. The level of hustle is almost nil."

"People here seem to truly care about others. The influence of the Church is strong. That's a big factor."

"Most people in the states have high aspirations. They want big houses, big cars, vacations homes. Here at Chapala the level of aspiration is much lower. People don't want big homes or yachts. They're satisfied with simple things in life. A modest home. A family. A steady job. That's why the stress level here is so low."

"I know many wealthy people who come here to beat stress."

"A good friend of mine--who happens to be a multi-millionaire--maintains a home in Chapala. He is semi-retired. His monthly income is between $30,000 and $40,000. He also maintains homes in Newport Beach,

A view of the beautiful mountains that surround Lake Chapala. The mountains take on a beautiful green and even purplish tone at certain times of the day. These beautiful mountains provide a nice backdrop to the blue Lake in the Chapala area.

These horses live wild around Lake Chapala. Nobody owns the horses. They just run wild and care for themselves.

California and Cabo San Lucas, Mexico. He could live any place in the world. But he chooses to spend 9 or 10 months every year here at Lake Chapala."

"The weather is the best in the world. There's no other place with this consistent kind of comfortable weather--both winter and summer."

"Many of my close friends living in Chapala are political refugees. One of my best friends is a refugee from Castro's Cuba. She moved here in 1958 when Castro took over. She, too, is well-to-do. She could live anywhere. Several others came here from South America to flee ruthless dictators. An elderly man in his 70's is a Jewish refugee from Hitler's Germany. These are the extremes."

"Most Americans at Lake Chapala live on a limited budget. Many of my close friends get by nicely on $300 a month or less. I know retired military families living on small pensions. Several couples live on very small Social Security checks. We all live comfortably. Things are cheap here. Money and material things don't mean that much."

"Many people visit here every year. Some have been visiting for 10, 15, 20 years or more. There must be a reason why intelligent people--who could live anywhere in the world--choose to come here to Lake Chapala."

"As a medical doctor I know the effect stress has on the body. It lessens the time you live."

We talked with this fascinating woman late into the night."

Heading For The Blue Pacific Waters

The Pacific ocean is just a few hours drive from Lake Chapala. There are many fine resorts on the Pacific.

The winter months from November to April are the best months to visit. The summer months can be very hot and uncomfortable. This is because the Pacific is at sea level. Sea level is great during the winter. But it's hot in the summer. There are two popular Pacific resorts near Lake Chapala--Puerto Vallarta and Manzanillo. Both can be reached by train, bus or car. Three other Pacific resorts are also nice to visit--but they are a little further away. These resorts and Mazatlan, Zihuatanego and Acapulco.

Puerto Vallarta

From Lake Chapala, Puerto Vallarta is about 260 miles away. You can get there by train, bus or air. Trains and buses run several times a day. Flights are available every hour from Guadalajara.

Puerto Vallarta is a small fishing village with a population of about 60,000. It was made famous by Richard Burton and Elizabeth Taylor. While filming a movie there, Richard and Liz began a romance. They liked Puerto Vallarta so much they bought two homes in the heart of town. The homes were on the same street across from each other. Richard Burton had a bridge built over the street to join the two homes. A gate separated the bridge. Richard and Liz spent many weeks vacationing at Puerto Vallarta during their long romance. When they broke up, Richard had a wall constructed to replace the gate. This symbolized the ending of their romance. Richard and Liz made Puerto Vallarta a fairly popular vacation spot. Before then, it was merely a quiet Mexican village.

Puerto Vallarta is an old Mexican seaport with cobblestone streets and red clay roofs. There are 2 sections of Puerto Vallarta: The older center of town and a newer addition that lies to the south of the main part of town. The center of town is noted for its little shops and fine restaurants. The newer section includes mainly large hotels built along the beach.

Puerto Vallarta is located on a large Bay--the second largest natural bay in the world. In the backdrop are rugged tropical mountains. The sunsets coming off the bay are among the most beautiful in the world. The red sunsets, blue water and colorful green mountains make Puerto Vallarta one of the most picturesque places in the world.

Prices in Puerto Vallarta are cheap. They are higher than Lake Chapala but by American standards they are still very low. For example, I stayed at a very nice hotel, right on the beach for about $10 a night. Food is also reasonable. Typically, you can expect to spend $3 to $4 for a good meal. Fish and seafood is especially inexpensive because Puerto Vallarta is a fishing village.

When visiting Puerto Vallarta I would recommend staying on the beach. There are many fine hotels off the beach. But the center of activity is on the beach. For example, most of the hotels have bars and restaurants a few feet away from the surf. They all provide shade in the form of overhead coverings and trees. Many people just lounge around enjoying the ocean. Roving mariachi bands travel up and down the beach from bar to bar. On any day you can enjoy as many as 10 or 15 roving bands. Each has a unique sound and style of entertainment.

Another attraction on the beach is the fresh fish. Local vendors grill it over charcoals right on the ocean. It makes a fine snack or meal. It's inexpensive and very good.

Another attraction on the beach is the kite ride. This costs about $5. Here's how it works: You are strapped to the kite at the end of a rope behind a motor boat. The motor boat picks up speed heading out towards the ocean. The kite gradually soars up toward the sky. The ride lasts about 15 minutes. It is fun.

Other entertainment in Puerto Vallarta includes horseback riding; sailing and fishing for sailfish, marlin or tuna.

When visiting Puerto Vallarta, take one of the local tours of the area. These tours last about 2 hours. They cover the entire town stopping at interesting historical points. Be sure to visit the area south of the main part of town. Many millionaires have large resort homes here. One of the biggest is the Wilson Sporting Goods home located near the ocean.

Where To Stay

The Hotel Rosita is one of the oldest hotels in the city. It's a popular place with Americans. It has a large beautiful pool and open-air bar that faces the ocean. The hotel was built in 1948 and was recently remodeled. The architecture is Spanish-Colonial. It is very pleasing. The hotel has about 100 rooms. The restaurant is on the ground floor. It is very good with reasonable prices.

Another nice hotel is the Rio. This hotel has much the same facilities as the Rosita but is smaller. The architecture is Spanish. The hotel is white with many beautiful trees and flowers on the grounds. It has a large pool with a bar that faces the ocean.

The Hotel Oceano is another popular American spot on the ocean. This hotel is famous for its well-patronized bar and central location. From the hotel you are within walking distance of any place in the town. The rooms are small with lots of Spanish wooden furniture. Most of the rooms have wood shutters. These

124

shutters can be adjusted to let more or less light in. Each room has a colorful Mexican bedspread. The hotel is constructed of stucco and dark wood. You can hear the surf at night from most of the rooms. This is especially soothing and conducive to restful sleep.

Where To Eat

The Los Cazuerlas is one of the most popular places to eat in Puerto Vallarta. This is a good place to sample the best of Spanish food. Most of the dishes are reasonable. It is open daily from noon to 11 p.m. Call for a reservation. There are only a few tables.

Another favorite restaurant is the La Iguana. It is only a couple of blocks from the river. Full dinners are very reasonable. This restaurant specializes in Chinese, Kosher, Mexican and American dishes. The owner was born in Mexico. His parents came here from China. This restaurant is primarily visited by tourists. Very few Mexicans eat here. The restaurant features entertainment from about 8 p.m. to 1 a.m.

Night Life

Many Americans go to the Hotel Oceano. A band plays there almost every night. You can listen or dance to Spanish music. Many students from the University of Guadalajara go here. Most of these students speak English. Other places to go for entertainment are Carlos O'Briens or Casablancas. Most of these lounges have good quality Spanish music. Drinks are reasonable.

What To Do During The Day

During the day many people spend a lot of time at the beach. You can also wander through the cobblestone streets stopping at the many fine shops selling unique Mexican handicrafts.

Manzanillo

Manzanillo is a tiny fishing village located on the Pacific. It has a population of about 35,000. Its main industries are fishing and tourism. The center of activity is the plaza in the heart of town. The plaza is very colorful with green trees and red flowers.

The major daytime attraction is the beaches. The best beach is the La Audiencia. It offers the best swimming. Another good beach is the San Pedrito. This beach is shallow--you can walk out a long way and still stand up. It is the most popular beach--right near downtown. Taxi cabs in this town do not have meters. It is a good idea to negotiate a price before hiring a cab.

Manzanillo is famous for its fishing. Many people visit here to fish for marlin, sailfish, dolphin, sea bass and manta ray. Fishing competitions are held in November and January.

Many charter boats are available at low rates. The rates usually include tackle and bait.

Every Sunday a band plays by the waterfront in the center of town. This area is called the Rombeolas. There is no charge to listen. There is a slight charge if you want to use the dance floor.

Where To Stay

There are three distinct areas of the city where you can stay. One is the downtown area. There you'll be near shops, markets and activity. Next is Playa Azul. This is a motel-lined beach just north of the city. Last is Santiago. This is a suburb on the northern end of Playa

Azul. All the areas are convenient to get to by bus or taxi.

A popular hotel in the downtown area is the Hotel Colonial. It is spotlessly clean with nicely furnished rooms.

On the Playa Azul is the Hotel La Posada. This is a quality hotel. The grounds are well maintained with plenty of large shade trees. The architecture is Spanish with pink stucco. The back has a large arc that looks out to the beach. The rooms are large with tasteful Mexican furnishings.

In Santiago a nice hotel is the Cassablanca Alamar. This is a clean hotel built around a central courtyard and pool. It has a back terrace that faces the ocean. This is a very quiet and isolated place. The owners are very friendly. There is a good restaurant on the premises.

Where To Eat

The El Sombrero is one of the cleanest restaurants in Mexico. The food is delicious and the prices are reasonable. This restaurant is open only in the evenings from 7 o'clock to midnight.

The Chantilly is a popular place. It has an international menu. The food is good and the prices are very cheap. You can get anything here from a hamburger to steak. The ice cream is very good.

Getting To Manzanillo

A train leaves from Guadalajara every morning at 10 a.m. The train arrives in Manzanillo at about 6 p.m. Aero Mexico has daily flights from Guadalajara. You can also get to Manzanillo by bus from Guadalajara.

Side Trips

Thirty-five miles northwest of Manzanillo is Melaque Bay. There are 3 small villages here: Melaque, San Patricio and Barrandenavidad. These tiny villages are a good place to relax and get sun. They are simple fishing villages. There is nothing really to do except relax. The largest of the 3 villages is San Patricio.

Other Pacific Coast Cities Near Lake Chapala

Mazatlan

Mazatlan is a fairly large resort town on the Pacific. The population is about 200,000. The fishing attracts people from the United States, Canada and other parts of the world. Because of its beautiful beaches and mild temperatures, Mazatlan is often referred to as the Pearl of the Pacific.

The main beach is right downtown. It is noted for its spectacular sunsets. Mazatlan is a great place to shop and get souvenirs. Many people visiting Mazatlan rave about the Fiesta Yacht Cruise. This large, double-deck boat leaves every morning at 10 a.m. from the south beach by the lighthouse. You can buy tickets from any of the large hotels. The cruise lasts about 3 hours going around the harbor and bay. A bi-lingual guide explains all the marine activities. A band will entertain you with Mexican music. The ship also stops several times so you can swim. Cooling drinks are served on the cruise.

Another delightful way to spend a day is to rent a fishing boat. You can rent boats on the south side of town. Rates are very reasonable.

Many people enjoy the scenery by renting a bicycle or motor scooter. This is one of the best ways to see the city. It is also one of the best ways to examine the outskirts of town.

Every Sunday you can enjoy bull fights in the city's main arena. Bull fights are only held in winter. Rodeos and other activities are presented other times of the year.

One of the main attractions in Mazatlan is a bar called Senor Frog. This bar is almost internationally known for its music and food. At night when the music gets going, people actually dance on the tables. This is always fun to watch.

Where To Stay

Generally, there are two classes of hotels in Mazatlan. One is in the main part of the city. These hotels are older and less expensive. The other class is by the beach. These hotels are newer and cost a little more.

The Hotel Belmar is a popular hotel located right on the waterfront. The hotel is very elegant with a Colonial-Spanish flavor. It is built around a beautiful courtyard. You enter the hotel through huge wooden gates. It has a new pool, tennis courts and other recreational activities. This hotel has lots of flowers and colorful tiles.

Another popular hotel is the Hotel La Siesta. This too, is located on the ocean. The rooms are large with balconies. The hotel has a fine restaurant with nightly entertainment. All rooms are air conditioned. This is important in the summer. In the winter you will not need air conditioning.

The Hotel Olas Atlas is a popular place to stay. Most rooms have an ocean view. The hotel has a nice balcony that overlooks the ocean.

Where To Eat

The Madrid has good food at reasonable prices. A few outdoor tables overlook the ocean. The restaurant is noted for its fruit salads and seafood.

Another popular restaurant for Americans is the El Shrimp Bucket in the Hotel La Siesta. The restaurant has live music and dancing.

Acapulco

There's nothing like Acapulco--it's one of a kind. It claims to be the pleasure capital of the world. It has perfect weather. The food ranges from American to authentic Mexican. Acapulco has all kinds of accomodations at all different prices. It has a population of about 600,000. Acapulco has often been compared to other enchanting places like the French Riviera. It is noted for its night life.

Acapulco is situated on a large bay. The town stretches all around the bay. Walking is not practical-- unless you like to walk. Taxis can get you around the city. They are inexpensive.

Many people enjoy cruising around the bay in the popular yacht called Fiesta. There are two cruises. One at about 4:30 p.m. The other is a moonlight cruise with music and dancing. Two other boats called the Sea Cloud and the Bonanza make similar trips daily.

Where To Stay

The Hotel Boca Chica overlooks Caletilla Beach. This is a 5-story hotel that sits on a hillside. There are beautiful lawns, terraces and a pool. The hotel's location provides a 180 degree panoramic view of the bay. All the rooms are air-conditioned. They are constructed in

130

marble and Mexican tile with lots of windows. The hotel has facilities for water-skiing, sailing, scuba diving, deep sea fishing, surfing, golf and tennis.

The Hotel Villa Rica is another popular hotel. This is a new hotel. Many rooms have balconies with bay views. All rooms are large with air-conditioning. The beds are large and firm. The hotel has a large, beautiful pool.

The Hotel Casino Hornos is a good place to stay. The hotel is 17 stories high. All rooms are air-conditioned. It has all the conveniences of a modern hotel. This hotel has a beautiful roof-top bar. There is also a nice bar on the beach. The restaurant is good too. It is right on the beach. You can get spectacular views of the bay.

Where To Eat

The Mariscos Pipo is a popular restaurant for seafood. You can get delicacies like octapus and snail at a relatively cheap price.

Zihuatanejo

This is a very fast-growing fishing village. In 1972 there were about 4,000 inhabitants. Today there are almost 20,000. This is a beautiful city. The beach curves around a small, beautiful bay. You can see fishing boats and sailing boats all around the bay. You get the feeling you've gone back in time 100 years. This is a good place to relax. Some of the better hotels are the Marina and the Casa Elvira. Both of these hotels are right on the beach.

Playa Azul

This city has a population of about 6,000. It is an off-beat tropical paradise. It faces the ocean rather than the bay like Acapulco. The town lies behind a row of magnificent cocoanut trees. This is a good place to relax. It is not noted for its entertainment.

Where To Stay

The Hotel Playa Azul is in the center of town. It has 56 rooms--all air-conditioned. The rooms are clean. The hotel has a pool.

Another popular hotel is the Hotel Laloma. It has 100 rooms, many with ocean views. Rooms have private balconies and air-conditioning. There is live entertainment on weekends. The hotel has a nice, large pool.

Where To Stay: A Partial List Of Lake Chapala Hotels

Hotel Real de Chapala

Telephone	:	5-24-16
Location	:	Ajijic
Rate	:	$20 double occupancy (more in December)
Pool	:	Yes
Restaurant	:	Yes
Bar	:	Yes

This is my favorite. A real first-class hotel located right on the shores of the Lake. Huge luxurious rooms complete with lounge area, couch, table and chairs. Hotel has complete facilities including large pool with outside bar, billiard game and T.V. room. Also has tennis courts, volley-ball court and ping-pong tables.

This hotel has two fine restaurants and a beautiful courtyard eating area that is perfect for lunch. Every Sunday the Hotel hosts an "old Mexico" style buffet complete with a mariachi band and authentic mexican dancers.

Hotel Chapala Haciendas

Telephone   : 5-27-20
Location   : Chapala
Rate   : $6 per person for room with kitchen
Pool   : Yes
Restaurant   : Yes
Bar   : Yes
Other   : Pool is surrounded by tropical garden setting. Dances every Wednesday and Saturday night. Located about 4 miles from the Lake on a hillside on the main road to Guadalajara.

Hotel Chula Vista

Telephone   : 5-22-13
Location   : Chapala
Rate   : $20 double occupancy
Pool   : Yes
Restaurant   : Yes
Bar   : Yes
Other   : This is an American style motel located on the main road that goes around the lake.

Monte Carlo

Location   : Chapala
Rate   : $22 double occupancy
Pool   : Yes
Restaurant   : Yes
Bar   : Yes
Other   : Large beautiful grounds with giant palm trees, a huge pool, and two tennis courts. Fronts the lake. Located just west of Chapala on the main road that goes around the Lake.

Hotel Nido

Telephone   : 5-21-16
Location   : Downtown Chapala
Rate   : $7 one person - $10 two persons
Pool   : Yes
Restaurant : Yes
Bar   : Yes
Other   : Built in the early 1900's by an American com-
              pany. This old spanish style hotel has high
              ceilings and pleasing design. Located near the
              Lake in downtown Chapala.

Apartments

Posada Las Calendreas

Telephone   : 5-28-19
Location   : Ajijic
Rate   : $9 for one - $14.50 for 4
Pool   : Yes
Restaurant : No
Bar   : No
Other   : The units surround a pool. Units are furn-
              ished with cooking facilities. Located on the
              lakeside of the main road going around the
              lake.

Las Casistas Apartments

Location   : Ajijic
Rate   : $155 a month
Pool   : No
Restaurant : No
Bar   : No
Other   : Located on main road that goes around the
              Lake.

Calle Hidalgo

Location	: Chapala
Rate	: $90 a month--one bedroom, $108--2 bedroom
Pool	: No
Restaurant	: No
Bar	: No
Other	: These units have large rooms. The 2-bedroom units have two baths, a living room and dining room. Kitchens have full cooking facilities.

Norman Apartments

Location	: Chapala
Rate	: $80 a month
Pool	: Yes
Restaurant	: No
Bar	: No

Trailer Park

Location	: Chapala
Rate	: $1.20 a day
Pool	: No
Restaurant	: No
Bar	: No
Other	: The most popular American style trailer court. Rates include full hookups plus purified water delivered daily. Located on the Lake off the main road that goes around the Lake.

Because of the daily peso devaluation and fluctuation in value of the dollar, rates are subject to change. Be sure to get current rates.

Basic Spanish--Just Enough To Get By

When traveling in Mexico it's a good idea to have an understanding of basic Spanish. In larger cities many Mexicans speak English, but fewer speak it in smaller towns.

It seems most problems occur in restaurants when you're ordering. That's why the basic Spanish I'm covering here emphasizes food and cooking instructions. Other Spanish words cover important signs and shopping.

Food Items

Main Food Items

bacon	tocino	toh-THEE-noh
beef	carne	KAHR-nay
cheese	queso	KAY-soh
chicken	pollo	POHL-yoh
egg	huevo	oo-AY-voh
fish	pescado	pays-CAH-doh
lobster	langosta	lahn-GOHS-tah
pancake	tortita de harina	tohr-TEE-tah deh ah-REE-nah
sausage	chorizo	choh-REE-soh
shrimp	camaron	cah-mah-ROHN
soup	sopa	SOH-pah
steak	filete	fee-LAY-tay
veal	ternera	tayr-NAY-rah

Vegetables, Etc.

bean	frijoles	free-HOH-lays
bread	pan	pahn
broccli	broculi	broh-COO-lee

butter	mantequilla	mahn-tay-KEY-yah
carrot	zanahoria	sah-noh-OH-ree-ah
catsup	salsa catsup	SAHL-sah
		CAHT-soop
cauliflower	coliflor	coh-lee-FLOHR
dressing	salsa	SAHL-sah
onion	cebolla	say-BOHL-yah
pea	guisante	gee-SAHN-tay
pepper	pimienta	pee-mee-AYN-tah
potatoe	papa	PAH-pah
salad	ensalada	ayn-sah-LAH-dah
salt	sal	sahl

How You Want Food Cooked

boiled	hervir	ehr-VEER
fried	frito	FREE-toh
grilled	parrilla	pah-REE-yah
hard	duro	DOO-roh
over	revolver	reh-VOHL-vehr
poach	escalfada	ess-cahl-FAH-dah
rare	poco asado	POH-koh
		ah-SAH-doh
soft	blando	BLAHN-doh
well done	bien cocido	bee-EHN
		coh-SEE-doh

Fruit

apple	manzana	mahn-SAH-nah
grape	uva	OO-bah
grapefruit	toronja	toh-ROHN-hah
juice	zumo	THOO-moh
orange	naranja	nah-RAHN-hah
pineapple	pina	PEE-nyah

Waiter Talk

bad	malo	MAH-loh
check	cuenta	coo-EHN-tah
cold	frio	FREE-oh
good	bueno	boo-EH-noh
hot	caliente	kah-lee-EHN-teh
how much	cuanto	koo-AHN-toh
ice	hielo	ee-AY-loh
menu	menu	meh-NOO
no	no	noh
tax	impuesto	eem-poo-AYS-toh
understand	comprender	kohn-prehn-DEHR
yes	si	SEE

Important Signs

careful	cuidadoso	koo-ee-dah-DOH-so
entrance	la entrada	lah ehn-TRAH-dah
exit	la salida	lah sah-LEE-dah
ladies room	damas	DAH-mahs
mens room	caballeros	kah-bah-YEH-rohs
no smoking	prohibido fumar	proh-ee-BEE-doh foo-MAHR
warning	aviso	ah-VEE-soh

Numbers

one	uno	ooh-noh
two	dos	dose
three	tres	trayss
four	cuatro	kwah-troh
five	cinco	seen-koh
six	seis	sayss
seven	siete	syeh-tay

eight	ocho	oh-choh
nine	nueve	nway-bay
ten	diez	dee-ess
eleven	once	ohn-say
twelve	doce	doh-say
twenty	veinte	bayn-tay
thirty	treinta	trayn-tah
forty	cuarenta	kwah-ren-tah
fifty	cincuenta	seen-kwen-tah
sixty	sesenta	say-sen-tah
seventy	setenta	say-ten-tah
eighty	ochenta	oh-chen-tah
ninety	noventa	noh-ben-tah
one hundred	cien	see-en

Colors

black	negro	NEH-groh
blue	azul	ah-SUL
dark	oscuro	ohs-KOO-roh
green	verde	VEHR-deh
light	claro	KLAH-roh
pink	rosa	ROH-sah
red	rojo	ROH-hoh
white	blanco	BLAHN-koh
yellow	amarillo	ah-mah-REE-yoh

Months

January	Enero	eh-NEH-roh
February	Febrero	feh-BREH-roh
March	Marzo	MAHR-thoh
April	Abril	ah-BREEL
May	Mayo	MAH-yoh
June	Junio	HOO-nee-oh
July	Julio	HOO-lee-oh
August	Agosto	ah-GOHS-toh

September	Septiembre	sehp-tee-EHM-breh
October	Octubre	ohk-TOO-breh
November	Noviembre	noh-vee-EHM-breh
December	Diciembre	dee-thee-EHM-breh

Days

Sunday	Domingo	doh-MEEN-goh
Monday	Lunes	LOO-nehs
Tuesday	Martes	MAHR-tehs
Wednesday	Miercoles	mee-EHR-koh-lehs
Thursday	Jueves	hoo-EH-vehs
Friday	Viernes	vee-EHR-nehs
Saturday	Sabado	SAH-bah-doh

Greetings

good day	buenos dias	boo-EH-nohs DEE-ahs
how are you	como esta usted	KOH-moh ehs-TAH oos-TEHD
good bye	Adios	ah-dee-OHS

Directions, Etc.

North	Norte	NOHR-teh
South	Sur	soor
East	Este	EHS-teh
West	Oeste	oh-EHS-teh
left	izquierda	eeth-kee-EHR-dah
right	derecha	deh-REH-chah
straight	recto	REHK-toh
beach	la playa	lah PLAH-yah
hill	colina	koh-LEE-nah
lake	lago	LAH-goh
map	mapa	MAH-pah
river	el rio	ehl REE-oh

140

| road | camino | kah-MEE-noh |
| valley | valle | VAH-yeh |

Fabrics

cotton	algodon	ahl-goh-DOHN
linen	lino	LEE-noh
rayon	rayon	rah-YOHN
satin	raso	RAH-soh
silk	seda	SEH-dah
wool	lana	LAH-nah

Miscellaneous

airport	aeropuerto	ah-eh-roh-poo-EHR-toh
bank	banco	BAHN-koh
doctor	doctor	dohk-TOHR
embassy	embajada	ehm-bah-HAH-dah
envelope	sobre	SOH-breh
gasoline	gasolina	gah-soh-LEE-nah
hospital	hospital	ohs-pee-TAHL
mechanic	mecanico	meh-KAH-nee-koh
police	policia	poh-lee-THEE-ah
post office	correos	koh-RREH-ohs
restroom	sanitario	sah-nee-TAH-ree-oh
stamp	sello	SEH-yoh
taxi	taxi	TAHK-see
telegraph	telegrafiar	teh-leh-grah-fee-ahr
telephone	telefono	teh-LEH-foh-noh

Mexicans are very helpful and courteous. They believe it's highly discourteous not to respond to a stranger asking a question. Because of this, a mexican may answer any question whether they know the answer or not. So be careful. You may think you're getting accurate information when you're not.

MENU
La Viude, Chapala

WELCOME

APPETIZERS		
MELTED CHEESE	$ 315.00
CHEESE TACOS (2)	,, 100.00
PIGS FEET	,, 350.00

SOUPS		
CREAM OF TOMATO	,, 130.00
CREAM OF MUSHROOM	,, 130.00
SOUP OF THE DAY	,, 130.00

— • —

FISH AND SEA FOOD

SHRIMP FILET	,, 820.00
SHRIMP DEVIL GAMBA CURRY	,, 730.00
WHITE FISH FROM THE LAKE WITH TARTAR SAUCE	,, 700.00
BREADED FILET OF SNOOK WITH TARTAR SAUCE	,, 660.00
RED SNAPPER TO YOUR TASTE	,, 660.00

— • —

STEAKS AND CHOPS

CHATEAUBRIAND (2 PERSONS)	,, 1,440.00
FILET MIGNON	,, 740.00
BLACK PEPPER STEAK	,, 770.00
T-BONE STEAK (400 GRMS.)	,, 660.00
NEW YORK STEAK	,, 590.00
EYE RIB STEAK	,, 480.00
PORK CHOPS WITH APPLE SAUCE	,, 470.00
SMOKED PORK CHOPS	,, 510.00
CHICKEN IN THE BASKET	,, 530.00
CHICKEN CURRY	,, 530.00
CHICKEN BREAST PARMESAN	,, 530.00
CHOPPED SIRLOIN STEAK, ONIONS RINGS	,, 380.00
SPAGHETTI WITH MEAT SAUCE	,, 380.00
BEEF TONGUE VERACRUZ STYLE O VINAGRET	690.00

THESE ORDERS ARE SERVED WITH SALAD
HELP YOURSELF FROM OUR SALAD BAR
FRENCH FRIES OR BAKED POTATOE,
 BREAD WITH GARLIC BUTTER.

— • —

THIN CUT MEATS

PORK SHANKS, CHARCOAL BROILED	,, 600.00
BEEF LOIN CHARCOAL, BROILED OR GRILLED	,, 480.00
SHISHKABOB	,, 480.00
PORK LOIN, CHARCOAL, BROILED OR GRILLED	,, 480.00

THESE ORDERS ARE SERVED WITH
HOT TORTILLAS AND HOT BEANS.

— • —

SANDWICHES

CLUB HOUSE 3 DECKER WITH FRENCH FRIES	,, 350.00
CHICKEN SANDWICH WITH FRENCH FRIES	,, 250.00
HAM SANDWICH WITH FRENCH FRIES	,, 250.00
HAMBURGUER WITH FRENCH FRIES	,, 250.00
CHEESE SANDWICH WITH FRENCH FRIES	,, 220.00

COCKTAILS

S H R I M P	,, 420.00
O C T U P U S	,, 420.00
O Y S T E R S	,, 420.00
M I X E D	,, 420.00

POSTRES

HOME MADE CAKE	,, 150.00
PECAN PIE	,, 150.00
C H O N G O S	,, 150.00
NAPOLITAN BREAD PUDDING	,, 150.00
PEACHES IN SYRUP	,, 150.00
ICE CREAM	,, 150.00

BEVERAGES

BEER ALL BRANDS	,, 160.00
COKE, ORANGE, SEVEN ETC.	,, 70.00
ICED COFFEE OR TEA	,, 50.00
COFFEE	,, 50.00

WINES

RED WINE ROSE WHITE LOS REYES BOT. ¾	,, 1,400.00
RED WINE ROSE WHITE ESCHENAUER BOT. ¾	,, 1,400.00
RED WINE SAN EMILION BOT. ¾	,, 1,400.00
MOSELLE STO. TOMAS BOT. 3/4	,, 1,400.00
DRY SAUTERNE WINE STO. TOMAS BOT. ¾	,, 1,400.00
GLASS OF WINE NACIONAL	,, 195.00

ENJOY OUR SALAD BAR   SERVE YOURSELF.
OPEN MONDAY FRIDAY FROM 8.00 TO 22 HS.   SATURDAY AND SUNDAY FROM 8 TO 2.00 A.M.
VISIT OUR BAR, DINING, DANCING EVERY SATURDAY AND SUNDAY FROM 9 P.M.

MENU
Hotel Real de Chapala, Ajijic

ALGO PARA EMPEZAR	**SOMETHING TO BEGINNING**

ALGO PARA EMPEZAR / **SOMETHING TO BEGINNING**

EL AGUACATE A LA REYNA
(relleno con pollo y salsa roja o Aurora)
AVOCADO QUEEN
(Filled with chicken and delicious sauce) — 300.00

EL COCKTAIL DE CAMARONES
(camarones frescos y salsa catsup)
SHRIMPS COCKTAIL
(with fresh shrimps and catsup sauce) — 450.00

LOS PALMITOS VINAGRETA
(palmitos con salsa vinagreta)
THE HEARTS OF PALM
(with vinagrete dressing) — 300.00

DE NUESTRA MARMITA / **FROM OUR LOCALE MARMITA**

LA SOPA DEL PESCADOR
(camarón, jaiba, pulpo, pescado y almeja)
FISH SOUP
(shrimps, various fishes, octopus and cleam) — 500.00

LA SOPA AZTECA
(la tradicional sopa de tortilla c/crema
y aguacate)
AZTECA SOUP
(the traditional tortilla soup with
cream and avocado) — 250.00

LA SOPA DE CEBOLLA
(gratinada con queso)
ONION SOUP
(topped with cheese) — 200.00

EL CONSOME AXIXIC
(con pollo, arroz y perejil)
AXIXIC BROTH
(served with strips of chicken, rice
and parsley) — 200.00

UN REFRESCANTE INTERMEDIO / **A REFRESHING IN BETWEEN**

LA ENSALADA DEL CHEF
(la clásica ensalada de jamón, queso amari-
llo y pollo c/aderezo de salsa Aurora)
CHEF'S SALAD
(the classic salad of ham, cheese,
and chicken with dressing) — 300.00

LA BARCA DE FRUTAS
(media piña c/frutas de la estación)
CANOE OF FRUITS
(1/2 pineapple with fruits of the season) — 300.00

LA ENSALADA MIXTA
(lechuga, chícharos, ejotes y aguacate
c/aderezo al gusto)
MIXED SALAD
(lettuce, peas, way beans and avocado
with dressing at your choice) — 200.00

LOS SANDWICHES / **SANDWICHS**

REAL CLUB SANDWICH
(el típico de jamón, tocino, queso y pollo)
REAL CLUB SANDWICH
(the tipical of ham, bacon,
cheese and chicken) — 300.00

HAMBURGUESA STEAK
(servida c/cebolla frita, tomate y
papa francesa)
HAMBURGER STEAK
(served with fried onions, tomato,
and french fried potatoes) — 350.00

SANDWICH DE JAMON Y QUESO
HAM AND CHEESE SANDWICH — 200.00

EL GRILL / **THE GRILL**

BROCHETA "AZULEJOS"
(trocitos de filete marinados, con
pimiento, tomate, tocino y cebolla
asada al carbón)
SHISKA BOB "AZULEJOS"
(marinated beef, green pepper, tomato,
bacon and onion charcoal style) — 600.00

NEW YORK CUT
(asado en la forma tradicional, al
carbón, servido con papa al horno)
NEW YORK CUT
(the traditional charcoal)
served with baked potatoes) — 800.00

FILETE MIGNON
(servido con papas francesas, vegetales
y champiñones)
MIGNON FILLET
(served with french fried potatoes
and mushrooms) — 1,000.00

POLLO A LA PARRILLA
(1/2 pollo servido con papa francesa)
CHICKEN GRILL
(1/2 chicken served with french potatoes) — 450.00

CHULETA DE CERDO
(con salsa de manzana)
PORK CHOPS
(with apple sauce) — 450.00

NUESTRO CHEF LE SUGIERE

SPAGHETTI "TUTO MARE"
(c/camarón, callo de hacha, champiñones
 bañados en salsa de tomate)
MAR Y TIERRA
(sólo para paladares exigentes; medallones
de filete de res y langosta)

OUR CHEF'S SUGESTION

SPAGHETTI "TUTO MARE" $ 600.00
(with shrimp, fish and mushrooms,
beathed in tomato sauce)
SURF AND TURF   3,000.00
(only for the demanding palates; strips
of beef and lobster toil)

DEL OCEANO PACIFICO

FILETE DE PESCADO A LA PARRILLA O AL AJO
(servido con salsa tártara y arroz)
CAMARONES GIGANTES AL AJILLO,
 A LA PLANCHA O EMPANIZADOS
(Servidos sobre arroz y acompañados
con verduras)

FROM THE PACIFIC OCEAN

FISH FILLET GRILL OR GARLIC   750.00
(served with tartare sauce and rice)
GIANT SHRIMP GARLIC,   1,600.00
GRILL OR BREADED
(served on a bed of rice and
accompanied with vegetables)

LA COMIDA MEXICANA

LAS TIPICAS ENCHILADAS POBLANAS
LOS TACOS DE CARNE
(blandos, servidos con guacamole, frijoles,
crema y queso)
LA TAMPIQUEÑA
(servida c/una enchilada, rajas de chile,
arroz, guacamole y totopos)

MEXICAN SPECIALS

TYPICAL ENCHILADAS POBLANAS   375.00
TACOS WITH MEAT   320.00
(bland served with avocado, mexican
beans, cream and cheese)
LA TAMPIQUEÑA   760.00
(served with one enchilada, slices of
pepper, rice, avocado, mexican beans
and tortilla chips)

LOS POSTRES

PAY DE QUESO CON FRESAS
PASTEL DE LA CASA
CREPAS A LA CAJETA
BANANA SPLIT
FLAN AL CARAMELO
GELATINA

DESSERTS

CHEESE PIE WITH STRAWBERRIES	150.00
HOUSE CAKE	80.00
SWEET CREPES	150.00
BANANA SPLIT	200.00
FLAN WITH CARAMEL	80.00
GELATIN	60.00

BEBIDAS

CAFE AMERICANO, NESCAFE O DECAF
TE CALIENTE O HELADO
MALTEADAS
LECHE
LIMONADA O NARANJADA
SANGRIA
COPA DE VINO
REFRESCOS
CERVEZAS
BEBIDAS A BASE DE LICORES NACIONALES

BEVERAGES

AMERICAN COFFEE, NESCAFE OR DECAF	60.00
HOT TEA OR ICE TEA	60.00
MALTS	120.00
MILK	60.00
LIMONADE OR ORANGEADE	100.00
SANGRIA	225.00
CUP OF WINE	160.00
SOFT DRINKS	50.00
BEER	150.00
BEVERAGES WITH NATIONAL LIQUOR	

MENU
Posada, Ajijic

Appetizers —

Shrimp Cocktail	380
Deep Fried Shrimp with Tartar Sauce	400
Melted Cheese with Sausage and Tortillas	360
Seafood Crepes	400
Ceviche Cocktail	320
Fruit plate	240

Soups —

Soup of the Day — Cup	170
Bowl	200
French Onion Soup with Melted Cheese	230
Azteca Soup	200

Salads —

Green Salad — French, 1200 Islands, Roquefort, or Italian Dressings	200

Entrees —

Plato Mexicano	570
T-Bone Steak — 350 gr. with Onion Rings	1,250
New York Steak — 275 gr.	1,250
Pepper Steak with Bernaise Sauce	1,100
Shish-Ka-Bob — Filet Tips	1,100
Huachinango — Plain	600
Garlic Butter	650
Veracruzano	650
Shrimp — Plain	1,450
Garlic Butter	1,500
Pernod	
Filet of Fish — Plain or House Sauce	600
Curried Shrimp with Condiments	700
Curried Chicken with Condiments	600
Breaded Veal with Tomato Sauce	550
Melted Cheese	625
Fried Egg	625
Butterfly Pork Chop with Apple Sauce	800
Chicken Breast with Bleu Cheese and Tarragon Sauce	1,200

— Above Served with Baked Potato, Rice, or French Fries—
—Vegetable of the Day — Bolillo and Butter—

Desserts —

Chocolate Sundae	150
Caramel Sundae	150
Ice Creams	130
Dessert of the Day	190

Drinks —

Coffee	60
Tea	60
Hot Chocolate	90
Glass of Milk	80
Lemonade	130
Orangeade	130
Iced Tea or Coffee	90

All Prices are Subject to a Tax of 15% Tax.

MENU
El Meson, Ajijic

To Start With

AVOCADO SALAD (Guacamole)	300
GREEN SALAD AU VINAGRETTE	300
MELTED CHEESE (For One Person)	600

Soups

"CONDE" SOUP (Beans)	300
CHICKEN BROTH	300
SHRIMP	500

Specialities

CHICKEN MIXIOTE	1,000
MEXICAN PLATE	1,000
GRILLED BEEF (Mexican Style)	1,000
BAR-B-Q PORK CHOPS	1,100
LOIN OF PORK (Mushroom Sauce)	1,200
SHRIMPS AU PARSLEY SAUCE	1,500
MIXED GRILL (For Two)	2,500

Desserts

CAKE	200
ICE CREAM	200
CUSTARD	200

Beverages

COFFEE OR TEA	100

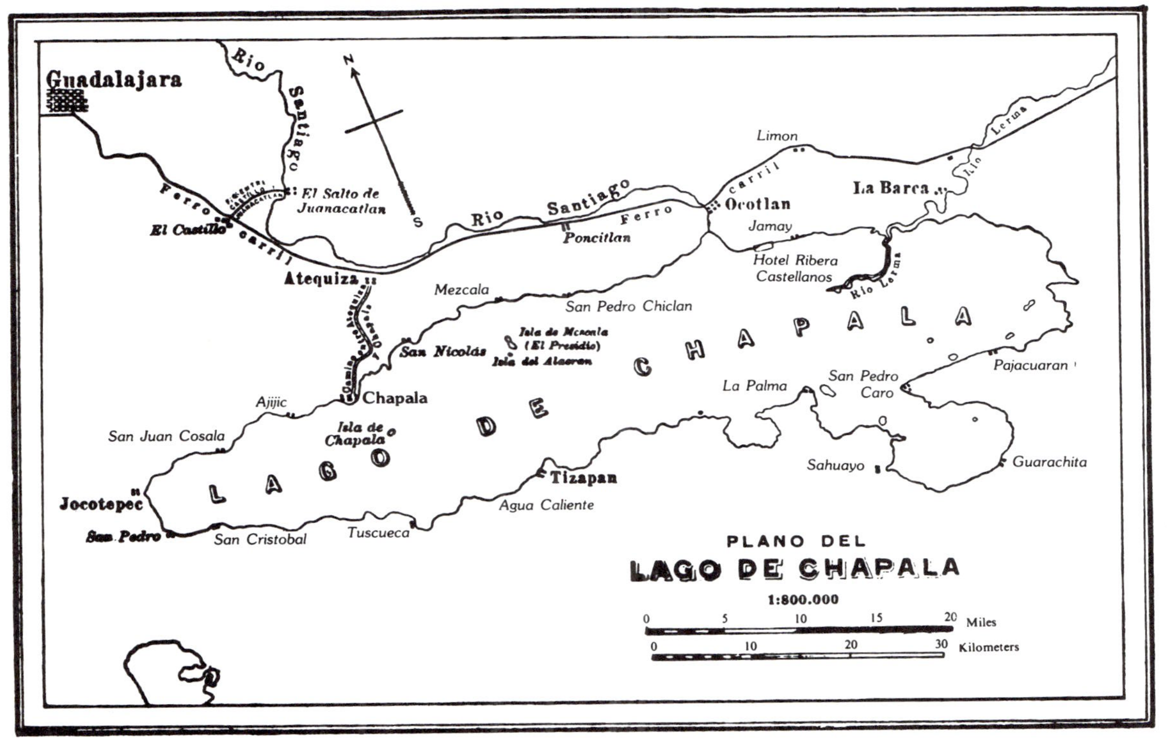

Guadalajara
Rio Santiago
N
S
El Salto de Juanacatlan
Ferro carril
El Castillo
Atequiza
Rio Santiago
Ferro
Poncitlan
carril
Limon
Ocotlan
La Barca
Rio Lerma
Jamay
Hotel Ribera Castellanos
Rio Lerma
Mezcala
San Pedro Chiclan
Isla de Menonia (El Presidio)
Isla del Alacran
San Nicolas
Ajijic
Chapala
Isla de Chapala
San Juan Cosala
LAGO DE CHAPALA
La Palma
San Pedro Caro
Pajacuaran
Sahuayo
Guarachita
Tizapan
Agua Caliente
Jocotepec
San Pedro
San Cristobal
Tuscueca
PLANO DEL
LAGO DE CHAPALA
1:800.000
0 5 10 15 20 Miles
0 10 20 30 Kilometers

MAP OF MEXICO